GOING
NATIVE

BIODIVERSITY
IN OUR OWN
BACKYARDS

Janet Marinelli ⚊ Editor

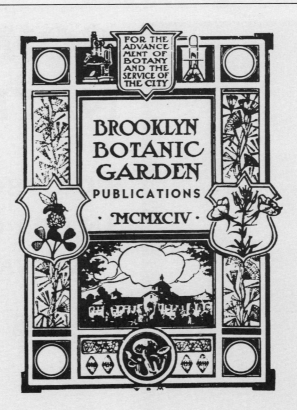

FOR THE
ADVANCE
MENT OF
BOTANY
AND THE
SERVICE OF
THE CITY

BROOKLYN
BOTANIC
GARDEN
PUBLICATIONS
· MCMXCIV ·

Janet Marinelli
EDITOR

Bekka Lindstrom
ART DIRECTOR

Stephen K-M. Tim
VICE PRESIDENT, SCIENCE & PUBLICATIONS

Judith D. Zuk
PRESIDENT

Elizabeth Scholtz
· DIRECTOR EMERITUS

Handbook #140

Copyright © Autumn 1994 by the Brooklyn Botanic Garden, Inc.

BBG gardening guides are published quarterly at 1000 Washington Ave., Brooklyn, NY 11225

Subscription included in Brooklyn Botanic Garden membership dues ($25.00 per year)

ISSN 0362-5850 ISBN # 0-945352-85-9

PRINTED IN KOREA

Table of Contents

WHAT IS A BIODIVERSE GARDEN?

BY JANET MARINELLI

GREW UP on Long Island on a block called Garden Place. Sounds like a perfect name for a horticultural soap opera, and ecologically it could have been scripted by Stephen King. Grandma grew tomatoes. Dad mowed the lawn. Every Mother's Day Mom got another pink azalea or the latest shade of creeping phlox. Today, my childhood home looks like just about every other suburban garden from Boston to Seattle, with its golf course-quality lawn, clipped yews, azaleas and shade trees ringed by begonias.

When Henry Hudson landed on Long Island in 1609, he sang the praises of its white ocean strands carpeted with beach plum and prickly pear. As more and more families like mine settled on Long Island, I watched the beach plum get trampled. Much of the ancient oak forest that blanketed the island's spine yielded to suburban sprawl. The Hempstead plains, once the largest prairie on the East Coast, today is virtually extinct; also extinct is the Eskimo curlew, a beautiful bird with a long, curved bill, which was once hunted there. But I never put two and two together. Only in the past few years have I realized what ecological devastation conventional gardening has wrought.

We are poised on the brink of an age of extinction, a disaster to rival anything in evolutionary history, including the mass extinction of the dinosaurs 65 million years ago. As wilderness shrinks and backyard acreage increases, the home gardener's role in this biological debacle grows ever greater. Across a continent of breathtaking diversity we've planted the same two or three dozen plants. No wonder botanists are concerned about the long-term survival of almost 4,300, about 20 percent, of this country's native species — plants that are critical habitat for countless other creatures.

Our gardens threaten biodiversity in other ways as well. Free of the checks and balances that controlled their numbers in their original lands, scores of imported plants have jumped the garden gate and swamped our native vegetation. Park and preserve managers struggle daily to control these invasive pests.

The U.S. Census Bureau calculates that the nation's suburbs have almost doubled in area in the past two decades, and 400 square miles are added every year. As suburbia encroaches on natural areas, there is less room for plants and animals. During the 1960s, scientists first recognized that smaller areas also hold fewer *kinds* of plants and animals. According to their best estimates, a tenfold decrease in area slashes species diversity in half.

As garden acreage increases, natural areas are not only growing smaller, but

BIODIVERSITY STATE BY STATE

The following is a list of the estimated number of native species of vascular plants in each state:

ALABAMA 2,420	LOUISIANA 2,090	OHIO 1,920
ALASKA 1,250	MAINE 1,490	OKLAHOMA 2,280
ARIZONA 3,250	MARYLAND 2,040	OREGON 2,930
ARKANSAS 2,170	MASSACHUSETTS ..1,650	PENNSYLVANIA ...2,030
CALIFORNIA 5,090	MICHIGAN 1,950	RHODE ISLAND ...1,350
COLORADO 2,640	MINNESOTA 1,720	SOUTH CAROLINA .2,190
CONNECTICUT 1,670	MISSISSIPPI 2,030	SOUTH DAKOTA ...1,400
DELAWARE 1,580	MISSOURI 1,890	TENNESSEE 2,110
FLORIDA 2,870	MONTANA 2,110	TEXAS 4,510
GEORGIA 2,760	NEBRASKA 1,460	UTAH 2,590
HAWAII 1,150	NEVADA 2,680	VERMONT 1,490
IDAHO 2,310	NEW HAMPSHIRE .1,420	VIRGINIA 2,320
ILLINOIS 2,060	NEW JERSEY 1,910	WASHINGTON 2,330
INDIANA 1,840	NEW MEXICO 2,810	WEST VIRGINIA ...1,730
IOWA 1,390	NEW YORK 2,190	WISCONSIN 1,620
KANSAS 1,690	NORTH CAROLINA .2,450	WYOMING 2,080
KENTUCKY 2,020	NORTH DAKOTA ..1,140	

Kartesz, J.T. 1992. Preliminary counts for native vascular plant species of U.S. states, *Biodiversity Network News*, 5(3)

also more isolated from each other. Habitat fragmentation threatens genetic diversity, another basic level of the diversity of life. When populations of a species are cut off from one another, they are unable to exchange genetic material and inbreeding occurs. One likely result is that future generations will be less able to adapt to changing conditions, whether possible global warming or an imported insect pest. Because genetic variation is the material from which new species evolve, another probable result is less biodiversity over the long haul.

Gardens have a much more immediate effect on genetic diversity. Many of the plants at nurseries are named cultivars, which are propagated asexually, usually from cuttings (not sexually, from seed), as that's the only way to preserve the characteristics of the parent plants, whether a compact growth habit or a certain color leaf. So when you buy, say, *Athyrium filix-femina* 'Fancy Fronds', a dwarf cultivar of lady fern, you are buying a clone — a plant that is genetically identical to every other specimen of 'Fancy Fronds' in existence.

A GARDEN THAT ACTS LIKE NATURE

The goal of conventional gardening is to create an idyllic picture, a place where plants bloom prodigiously amidst expanses of perpetually green lawn. We urge our little patches of paradise to grow, grow, grow and bloom, bloom, bloom with continuous infusions of fertilizer and water. Then, with puritanical zeal, we

thwart their sex drives by mowing and deadheading, lest seed from a single plant scatter promiscuously across the land.

Granted, ever since the 18th century when tastemakers began to rail against formal landscapes in which virtually anything green was sheared into lollypops, poodles and peacocks, western gardens have become increasingly natural looking. English designers created a new landscape ideal of trees and grass — which suburban gardeners here have devotedly adopted. But it's no longer good enough to create gardens that *look* like nature. As the poet Frederick Turner has pointed out, we must create gardens that *act* like nature, that do what nature does. What nature does is reproduce itself, copy itself into the future, gradually improving on the copies by the evolutionary forces of sexual reproduction, mutation and selection. In order to act like nature, a garden must consist of plants that are suited to the conditions on the site and can thrive with minimal intervention by us. (However, they must not be invasive thugs.) One of the best things about most biodiverse gardens is that, once established, they require little maintenance. Our job as gardeners is to combine plants in "commu-

Left to right: A field of California poppies, bison in short-grass prairie, lupine in the Columbia River gorge, the Sonoran Desert in Arizona. Across a continent of breathtaking biological diversity, we've planted the same two or three dozen plants in our gardens.

nities" that enable them to form the sorts of mutually beneficial relationships with other plants and animals that allow them to prosper and reproduce. Then we should let a thousand seedheads shatter, confident that our horticultural creations will add over time to the exquisite forms of life that comprise biodiversity.

Because centuries of gardening the old way have made it hard for us to visualize the new ecological gardens, I asked some of this country's top native landscape designers to create a sample garden for the typical piece of property in their regions, complete with a landscape plan. From a biodiverse garden for the Long Island pine barrens to one for the California foothills, these landscapes include a diversity of species in a variety of habitats. They perform the vital task of re-creating the rich ecology of native plant communities that are disappearing from our land and our lives.

By now you're probably thinking that I've gone bonkers. What has the world come to when you can't even plant a perennial border without being politically incorrect? A few proponents of native landscaping are indeed biological extremists who consider all humans ecological outlaws and planting exotics a form of environmental treason. Hogwash. In the biodiverse garden, humans are a part of nature, not apart from it. A biodiverse garden includes plantings that celebrate our own species' long and fruitful relationship with the land, from elegant herb gardens accented with topiary spirals to patios edged with fragrant flower borders. And there's certainly room in our gardens for healthy, home-grown food. But these traditional plantings belong close to the house, and our natural habitat gardens toward the edges of our properties.

Someday we'll know enough about ecology to be able to create new plant communities combining species from around the globe that add to, rather than subtract from, Earth's wonderful diversity of life forms. We don't know how to do that yet. Our current system of scattered nature preserves in a larger suburban landscape is not working as a biological safety net. Chances are slim that much more American land will be cordoned off as wilderness to provide threatened species with ample living space. That means we gardeners have an important role to play in efforts to re-create the native habitats we have been destroying.

Imagine the possibilities: a new landscape in which biodiverse gardens link up to form a network of corridors that crisscross the continent, connecting nature preserves so that animals can move freely and plant seeds can disperse. Planting these gardens can be our great gift to the planet.

CREATING A GARDENER'S EDEN

BY JANE SCOTT

WE GARDENERS like to think of ourselves as being in tune with nature, yet how can we view the endless sheared lawns and clipped shrubbery that now blanket our landscapes without being plagued by nagging doubts? Where is the drama of the changing seasons? Where are the birds and butterflies? Where, in fact, is the regional landscape that once defined our very roots?

The Earth is in serious trouble. Everywhere, biodiversity is disappearing. Our landscape is now so fragmented that even preserving every remaining natural area would not be enough. No ecosystem can thrive in isolation; if its plants and animals are to survive long term, they must have avenues of contact with others of their kinds.

The good news is that *gardens* can provide such avenues. Of course, it is impossible for any man-made landscape to reproduce all the integrity and complexity of an unspoiled ecosystem. Nevertheless, creating gardens that reflect some of the richness of this country's disappearing woods, fields, deserts and prairies cannot help but improve the lots of many native plants and animals.

Unfortunately, there is a widespread impression that one must choose between a biodiverse garden and a beautiful one; that to be ecologically sensible one must live among weedy lots and ragged lawns. Not true. The idea is not simply to allow what will happen to happen, but to actively create the casual, integrated harmony that is found in nature.

In nature, as in human life, harmony depends on healthy communities. An ecological garden, therefore, is one that is built around a particular plant community. This is a revolutionary idea to many gardeners used to selecting plants for purely ornamental reasons and combining them in ways that have little relation to their original habitats. Yet it is one with enormous appeal to those of us who long to help the world environment.

The earth's natural vegetation is divided into large areas of forest, grassland and desert called Plant Provinces. Each is a plant community on a grand scale, yet each also has many smaller communities within its borders. For instance, the great sea of grass that once covered the central part of this country included both tall- and short-grass prairies as well as riverside communities. In the same way, different groups of plants predominate in "cold" and "hot" deserts of the West, and the kinds of trees found in forests vary according to site and exposure. This natural diversity is further complicated by "succession," meaning the plants presently growing on a previously disturbed site will be replaced over time. All these plant communities, large, small, successional and climax, are determined by soil type, topography, available water and extremes of temperature — the same factors you will consider when making your garden.

Creating an ecological garden, while not easy, can be profoundly satisfying. The aim is to create a private haven for your family that also provides space and support for all the interacting plants and animals that make up a viable natural community.

There are, of course, many ways to create a biodiverse landscape. City

A biodiverse garden is built around a plant community. The earth's natural vegetation is divided into large areas of forest, grassland and desert called Plant Provinces. Each is a plant community on a grand scale and includes many smaller communities.

KEY TO MAP

A Ice
B Arctic Tundra
C Boreal Forest
D Pacific Coastal & Cascade Mountain Forests
E Palouse Prairies
F Great Basin Desert
G California Forests & Alpine Vegetation
H California Grasslands, Chaparral and Woodlands
I Mojave and Sonoran Deserts
J Rocky Mountain Forests & Alpine Vegetation
K Central Prairies & Plains
L Eastern Deciduous Forests
M Chihuahuan Desert
N Coastal Plain Forests
O Tropical Forests

Adapted from *North American Terrestrial Vegetation*, edited by Michael G. Barbour and William Dwight Billings (New York, Cambridge University Press, 1988)

PLANT PROVINCES OF NORTH AMERICA

gardeners can simply add a few choice natives that are attractive to wildlife to a traditional plan, while in the suburbs, you may opt to reintroduce a piece of the neighborhood's original landscape. Those in more rural surroundings may find they can release an existing community from the grip of alien shrubs and vines by eliminating invasive plants, encouraging others and adding a few as they go along. The following are a few general guidelines for natural landscapers.

@ **Keep the high-maintenance areas close to the house, and plant the natural garden toward the periphery of your property.** Many of us will also want to have a place for traditional garden flowers, herbs or vegetables. Fine — just keep them near the house and increase the degree of wildness as you move outward through the garden. If you need more privacy for the terrace or to screen out an unattractive view, you'll find native plant communities can perform these practical functions as well as traditional exotics can.

@ **Reduce the size of your lawn.** Think of lawn as outdoor living space and keep only as much as you will need. Westerners in very dry areas can usually do away with grass altogether, whereas easterners may find that replacing the front lawn with shrubs, trees, ferns and wildflowers will support more wildlife as well as provide privacy and seasonal interest. In other areas, a low-maintenance prairie or field may be the best choice. If so, keeping the edges mown and cutting paths through the tall grass will make it look groomed rather than neglected.

@ **Get to know your land.** Examine your site carefully, noting the exposure of slopes to sun and prevailing winds as well as the location of any slow-draining areas. Plot the path of sunlight in all seasons of the year. Where is the deepest summer shade and the warmest sun in winter? Is your soil predominantly clay or sand, acid or alkaline? While it is true that a healthy soil is the first requirement for a healthy garden, it does not need to be overly rich; many attractive native communities grow on poor sandy soil. The point is to select plants that are ecologically appropriate for your particular situation. For instance, southern gardeners can choose from a rich native flora well adapted to high heat and humidity, while those in desert areas will find that indigenous plants will thrive without constant watering.

As soon as you have decided on the appropriate community for your garden, go into the field and study it. Pick out a group of plants that seems especially attractive to you, and analyze the lines, forms, colors and textures that make up its underlying pattern. Observe how certain clumps of shrubs and trees create peninsulas or hidden clearings, how edges are rarely abrupt but rather intermingle and blend into

One way to promote biodiversity: replace a patch of your lawn with a meadow of wildflowers and grasses. Above: Texas bluebonnet and Indian paintbrush.

one another. Note, too, which species clothe a hillside and which grow along the floodplain of a stream, keeping in mind the high and low spots on your lot.

Notice the shapes and growth habits of the plants that contribute most to a scene's appeal. You may be surprised to discover that the design you like is dominated by a relatively few species. For instance, the pervading character of a dry oak woods, with its understory of huckleberry and laurel, is subtly different from a woods of tulip poplar and dogwood. In an old field that is reverting back to forest, sumac and sassafras form large rounded thickets, while an upright red cedar provides a strong vertical accent.

By now, it will be obvious that designing a garden based on regional native landscapes requires an intimate knowledge of plants. You need to be able to recognize wild species, both native and non-native, at all stages of growth and at all times of the year. This is particularly true for gardeners who are trying to reclaim a neglected field or a young woods from the grip of invasive exotics.

You must also decide whether you want your garden to evolve into something else, or represent a certain stage of succession indefinitely. On a bare lot, for instance, one way to accommodate growth and change might be to plant a grove of young trees and surround them with native grasses and field flowers, introducing shade-loving woodland ferns and wildflowers as the trees grow and their tops intertwine. Or, you could arrest this natural succession by planting only smaller trees such as hawthorn, dogwood or red cedar and mowing periodically to keep out invading woody vegetation. If yours is a very small garden, try pruning a few native viburnums to resemble small trees and surround them with ferns or groundcovers.

◉ **Inventory the plants already growing on your land. Add native plants attractive to wildlife.** Take a hard look at the plants already growing on your lot. Decide which will stay, which should go and which can be moved to another location. Don't be shy about this; all true gardens are in a constant state of renewal. On the other hand, unless they show signs of being invasive, there is no reason why some existing exotics cannot be incorporated into your new design. However, when it comes to plants attractive to wildlife, it *is* important to stick only to natives. Birds and animals spread the seeds of the fruits they eat, making them largely responsible for the scourge of invasive aliens that is now choking out native vegetation virtually everywhere.

◉ **Plant in groups.** When it comes to the actual planting plan, think in terms of groups or natural associations of plants instead of a single shrub or tree. Use color-coded stakes — one color for trees, another for shrubs — and outline the groupings with nylon cord. At first, consider only the shapes and sizes of the plants you want: a tall narrow tree here, a more rounded one there or a screen so many feet high. (Remember, you must allow ample room for the mature size of each tree or shrub that will form the bones of your garden, even if the actual plant you install is only three feet high.) At the same time, try to imitate natural relationships: the four layers of a healthy woods, for instance (canopy, understory trees, shrubs and groundcovers), or the intermingling swaths of shrubs, flowers and grasses that are found in a high-quality field. Remember, too, that layered plantings are most attractive to birds, many of which sing, nest and feed at different levels.

Then, choose plants for the cover and food they provide as well as for the beauty of their flowers and foliage so that wild creatues can live and reproduce in your garden. Shun insecticides, and allow room for the insects, leaf litter and dead wood many birds and animals need. Let a few herbaceous plants go to seed, and remember to include larval food plants for butterflies as well as fragrant flowers.

If you follow these guidelines, your garden will not only celebrate each passing season with a variety of form, fruit and flowers, but also will be filled with dancing butterflies, lilting bird song and the hum of bees. Truly, it will be a garden that feeds both the earth and the soul. ◉

ACQUIRING NATIVE PLANTS

Biodiversity isn't just threatened by development and invasion of exotic species. Many plants are imperiled by collectors who dig them from the wild. To avoid wild-collected plants, buy only from nurseries that advertise that they propagate the plants they sell.

Plants that are difficult or slow to propagate are most vulnerable to digging. These include:
- Woodland wildflowers, particularly trillium and other members of the lily family
- Plants adapted to specialized habitats, such as orchids and bog plants
- Native terrestrial orchids, which are especially threatened as they have yet to be propagated successfully in commercial quantities
- Mature specimens of certain cacti
- Plants that produce few seeds
- Plants with strict cultural requirements

To avoid contributing to this problem, gardeners should consult a reliable guide, such as *The Gardener's Guide to Plant Conservation* (World Wildlife Fund and the Garden Club of America, 1993), before buying. Learn also to recognize the signs of a wild-collected plant. They are:
- Roots that have been compressed into a pot
- Soil in the pot different from that on the roots
- Leaves that are skewed and irregular

Buy plants grown from seed, because they do more to promote biodiversity than named cultivars, which usually are vegetatively propagated clones of the parent plant. There are a few instances in which clones may be preferable — for example, those that are especially resistant to an imported disease or insect pest. Also, if you see named cultivars of species threatened by collection, it's a safe assumption that these have been propagated vegetatively, not dug up from the wild.

BIODIVERSITY
IN THE
BARRENS

BY KAREN BLUMER

HAT DO YOU DO when the bulldozer has carved out more than just a spot for the house on the site you had hoped would provide a natural setting and a refuge for wildlife? You do what one couple on the east end of Long Island plans to do: turn the ecological loss into an opportunity by drawing the remaining natural landscape into the garden design, while restoring native habitat in much of the cleared area.

The site is in the Long Island pine barrens, formed by the receding glaciers that covered much of North America thousands of years ago. The glaciers left well-drained, poor, sandy soils, which were colonized by pitch pines, scrubby oaks and an understory of blueberry, huckleberry and other members of the heath family, such as bearberry and wintergreen. Pine barrens are found only in the United States scattered in patches from New Jersey to Cape Cod.

Long Island's pine barrens, like those in New Jersey, have been under constant development pressure for decades. A reservoir of pure drinking water for the island's large semi-urban population lies beneath the ecosystem. The challenge has been one of sustainable growth: Is it possible to develop in the pine barrens and manage to preserve its ecological integrity and the drinking water beneath it? Long Island's pine barrens management plan centers on preserving a core area of 53,000 of the 100,000 acres designated officially as pine barrens, and controlling growth in the remaining 47,000 acres. In the zones slated for controlled growth, one way to protect biodiversity is to limit clearing. A second way, on sites that have already been bulldozed, is to restore native plant communities. The landscape plan on page 18 illustrates both approaches.

The site, located in Southampton, is a relatively high and dry pine-dominated forest to the north, changing to a richer oak-dominated forest as it slopes slightly to the south. On the southeast side, it dips, and the pine and oak habitats intergrade into a red maple and tupelo swamp. When the property was bulldozed, some trees remained. The original soils are also largely intact.

The owners want a landscape that is low-maintenance. For now, they want a modicum of lawn where their two children can play. Because Lyme disease is a problem in the area, they want a larger, tick-free area beyond the lawn. They also want a beautiful landscape based on native plant communities, both to create a refuge for wildlife and to preserve the character of the pine barrens location.

A BIODIVERSE GARDEN FOR THE PINE BARRENS

Long Island's pine barrens, like those in New Jersey, have been under constant development pressure for decades. Homeowners can help protect biodiversity by restoring native plant communities. This plan knits surrounding pine and oak woodlands and a red maple and tupelo swamp into the garden design. Eight other habitats have been added, including a meadow, a perennial wildflower border, several plantings of blueberry and other pine barrens shrubs, a series of cascading ponds and a low-maintenance lawn.

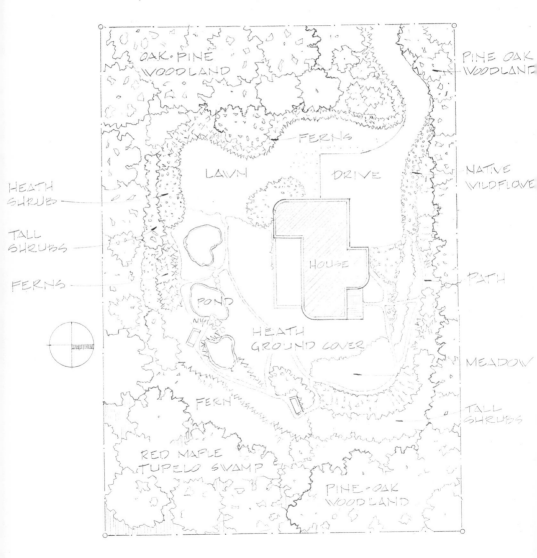

SELECTED NATIVE PLANTS

PINE-OAK AND OAK-PINE FORESTS:
Pitch Pine *Pinus rigida*
Black Oak *Quercus velutina*
Scarlet Oak *Q. coccinea*
White Oak *Q. alba*
Sassafras *Sassafras albidum*
American Beech *Fagus grandifolia*
Hickories *Carya* species

SWAMP:
Red Maple *Acer rubrum*
Tupelo *Nyssa sylvatica*
Spicebush *Lindera benzoin*
Red Chokeberry *Aronia arbutifolia*
Swamp Azalea *Rhododendron viscosum*
Jewelweed *Impatiens biflora*
Joe-pye Weed *Eupatorium dubium*
Wild Lily-of-the-valley *Maianthemum canadense*
Cinnamon Fern *Osmunda cinnamomea*
Royal Fern *Osmunda regalis*
Sensitive Fern *Onoclea sensibilis*
Skunk Cabbage *Symplocarpus foetidus*

TALL-SHRUB HABITAT:
Shadbush *Amelanchier canadensis*
Mountain Laurel *Kalmia latifolia*
Swamp Azalea *Rhododendron viscosum*
Chokeberry *Aronia* species
Elderberry *Sambucus canadensis*
Sassafras *Sassafras albidum*
Arrowwood *Viburnum dentatum*
Maple-leaf Viburnum *V. acerifolium*

LOW- AND MEDIUM-HEIGHT SHRUB HABITATS:
Bearberry *Arctostaphylos uva-ursi*
Wintergreen *Gaultheria procumbens*
Lowbush Blueberry *Vaccinium angustifolium*
Trailing Arbutus *Epigaea repens*
Huckleberry *Gaylussacia baccata*
Partridge Pea *Chamaecrista fasciculata*
Sweetfern *Comptonia peregrina*
Sheep Laurel *Kalmia angustifolia*

HERBACEOUS GROUNDCOVERS:
Bracken Fern *Pteridium aquilinum*
Wild Sarsaparilla *Aralia racemosa*
Wild Lily-of-the-valley *Maianthemum canadense*
Cinnamon Fern *Osmunda cinnamomea*
Lady Fern *Athyrium filix-femina*
Royal Fern *Osmunda regalis*
Sensitive Fern *Onoclea sensibilis*

MEADOW:
Little Bluestem *Schizachyrium scoparium*
Atlantic Golden Aster *Pityopsis falcata*
New York Aster *Aster novae-angliae*
Stiff Aster *A. linearifolius*
Bushy Aster *A. dumosus*
Golden Aster *Chrysopsis mariana*
Bird's-foot Violet *Viola pedata*
Butterfly Weed *Asclepias tuberosa*
Goldenrods *Solidago* species
Hyssop-leaved Thoroughwort
Eupatorium hyssopifolium
Goat's Rue *Tephrosia virginiana*
Blue Wild Lupine *Lupinus perennis*
Virginia Rose *Rosa virginiana*

PLANT COMMUNITY APPROACH

The key to the garden plan is designing not just with native plants, but with native plant communities — associations of species as they occur naturally in the wild. To increase the diversity of habitat types, the plan relies not only on mature oak, pine and swamp woodlands but also on successional plant communities — those that would evolve naturally in cleared areas of the pine barrens, such as those created by fire or windstorms, beginning with a low heath groundcover or a meadow and developing into shrubland and eventually woodland.

The disturbed woodland on either side of the front drive will be restored to the original pine-oak forest, featuring pitch pine and white, scarlet and black oaks, with bracken fern and lowbush blueberry growing underneath. A border of early- and late-blooming perennial wildflowers common in the sunny, open, sandy pine barrens flanks both sides of the drive. Medium-height heath shrubs provide an intermittent backdrop to the wildflower border, drawing the eye toward the restored woodland. The wildflower border offers season-long bloom, beginning with trailing arbutus (April), bird's-foot violet (May), blue wild lupine (May-June), goat's rue (June-July) and ending in the fall with golden asters, hyssop-leaved thoroughwort and goldenrods. The shrubs, including lowbush blueberry and huckleberry, provide food for songbirds, butterflies and small mammals.

The lawn comes into view on the right as you proceed up the driveway toward the house. Across the lawn to the south is a continuous fringe of bracken fern with large patches of wild sarsaparilla. Easing the transition to the oak-pine woodland beyond are intermittent islands of medium-height shrubs, mainly the three-foot-high sheep laurel, which is common in both the dry and moist pine barrens and features bright rose blooms in June. Behind them are tall evergreen mountain laurels, both pink- and white-flowering forms, which also bloom in June.

The lawn ends in a low-maintenance, evergreen — and, in my experience, tick-free — carpet of bearberry, which dominates the entire sunny south and

Right: Pitch pines, scrubby oaks and an understory of blueberry and other members of the heath family grow in the poor, sandy soils of the pine barrens. Meadows grow naturally in areas cleared by fire or windstorms.

eastern portion of the site around the house. A series of three lined ponds leads down the slope from the lawn toward the wetland and two sitting areas with benches. The ponds are linked by lined, rock-filled channels where gravity flow creates a continuous cascade of water — an excellent attraction for migrating songbirds, warblers and hummingbirds.

From the southernmost bench you can view the three ponds and hear the running water, which is returned to the top pond via a small pump. Native white pond lilies fill the first and third ponds; purple pickerelweed and white arrowhead, the middle pond. Cinnamon and sensitive ferns surround the bench, and a carpet of wild lily-of-the-valley leads the eye toward the swamp. This intimate sitting area is screened from the house by shrubs, including viburnums, which feature showy white flowers from mid-May through early June, and elderberry, which flowers just as the viburnums fade. Both shrubs produce huge clusters of black berries, providing excellent food and cover for songbirds, especially thrushes during migration. Behind and alongside these shrubs are beautiful native white swamp azaleas and chokeberry shrubs. Just to the northeast is the second bench, also surrounded by ferns and screened from the house by high shrubs, including viburnums, swamp azaleas, and shadbush, which all thrive in this semi-moist environment. A small stand of lavender-flowered joe-pye weed sets off a bush of brilliant orange-flowered jewelweed, both blooming in late summer.

From this sanctuary area, you can take a path north through the tall shrubs to the meadow, dominated by the native little bluestem grass. The grassland is dotted with colorful wildflowers, including orange butterfly weed, white hyssop-leaved thoroughwort, blue asters and goldenrods. Where the meadow meets the bearberry groundcover there is a generous mix of yellow-flowered partridge pea and golden asters. To the north and east, low heath groundcovers and taller shrubs blend the meadow into the pine-oak forest.

To the three existing habitats on the site — pine and oak woodland and swamp — eight others have been added: a low heath groundcover (bearberry, wintergreen, partridge pea); a perennial wildflower association for early and late bloom; a meadow; a medium-height heath shrub habitat dominated by huckle-berry, blueberries and sweetfern shrub; a tall-shrub habitat mixing dry upland and wet species and providing cover and food for migrating birds; an herbaceous groundcover, including wet and dry loving ferns and wild sarsaparilla; and two, more human-oriented habitats, a lawn and a series of cascading ponds.

LADY FERN

LOWBUSH BLUEBERRY

Arrowwood
Viburnum dentatum
A full, bushy shrub 6' to 15' tall. Dark green, heavily toothed leaves turn deep red in fall. Showy, creamy white flowers in flat-topped clusters in June. Black berries in late summer are a valuable food source for songbirds, especially thrushes. Also an important plant for butterfly larvae. Likes moist soil, semi-shade.

Lowbush Blueberry
Vaccinium angustifolium
Valuable low shrub groundcover to 1'. Light green leaves turn scarlet to orange in fall. White urn-shaped flowers in profusion in May. Luscious berries by July are a delight for both humans and wildlife, especially song-birds, butterflies and mammals, including fox. Will do well in sun or shade.

Lady Fern
Athyrium filix-femina
Woodland fern with graceful, feathery, light-green fronds. Excellent groundcover to about 2'. Spreads slowly. Very common in Long Island's wet woods, thickets, swamp edges. Tolerates shade to screened sun. Prefers moist, slightly acid soil.

![MOUNTAIN LAUREL]

MOUNTAIN LAUREL

PITCH PINE

Mountain Laurel
Kalmia latifolia

Shrub growing to 15' tall, with shiny dark evergreen leaves. One of the glories of Long Island in early June, when hilly stretches of oak-dominated forest are covered with spectacular swathes of its pink flowers. Also a rarer white-flowering form. Prefers the acid, moist but well-drained soil of craggy, morainal hillsides.

Pitch Pine
Pinus rigida

The most common tree on Long Island. Grows to 60' or more. Picturesque rough bark. Crown often sparse with strongly horizontal-growing branches that droop gracefully with age. Does well in dry, sandy to rich, wet acid soils. Seeds in the cones are eaten by a variety of birds and small mammals.

Bearberry
Arctostaphylos uva-ursi

Superb evergreen groundcover for dry, sunny areas. 6" to 8" high. Drooping, pink to white, waxy, bell-shaped flowers in May. Bright red berries in July. An important source of food for larvae of the hoary elfin butterfly. The berries are eaten by gamebirds, especially grouse, and some songbirds.

Blue Wild Lupine

Lupinus perennis

Lovely lavender to blue flowers typical of the pea family on spikes 1' to 2-1/2' high. Source of food for the larvae of orange sulphur and frosted elfin butterflies (and, upstate, the endangered Karner blue butterfly). Its long taproot makes it impossible to transplant, but it's very easy to propagate from seed.

New England Aster

Aster novae-angliae

Showy tall aster growing to 3' to 7'. Clusters of lavender, pink or violet flowers in late summer and fall. Common in Long Island's wet thickets, meadows and marsh margins. Also easy to grow in sun in average garden soil.

Hyssop-leaved Thoroughwort

Eupatorium hyssopifolium

Found in open woods and clearings. 1' to 3' tall perennial. White, bushy-topped flowers from August through November. Beetles, flies and migrating butterflies feed on the flowers. Thrives in full sun in dry to moist soils. Excellent candidate for the meadow or perennial border.

NEW ENGLAND ASTER

BLUE WILD LUPINE

A TASTE OF
THE
AMERICAN
SUBTROPICS

BY GEORGIA TASKER

EDWING BLACKBIRDS balance on the slender stalks of marsh plants like the Flying Wallendas. Both pond cypress and bald cypress frame the dock, and pop ash, swamp maple and pond apple grow at water's edge. Enormous leather ferns and clumps of beach lilies mingle at the base of slender paurotis palms.

You'd expect to find this scene in the Everglades, not in suburban Miami. Nonetheless, the small wetland garden, a transitional planting of dahoon hollies, buttonwood and coco plum and a tropical hardwood hammock on higher, drier ground are several decades old and have survived four freezes in the 1980s, three years of drought from 1988 to 1991 and Hurricane Andrew in 1992. Almost all of them were planted by Chirley Forthman and her late husband Hugh.

I visited this garden many years ago, and its ruggedly handsome character settled into my memory as a yardstick against which other efforts are measured. It offers a taste of what the real South Florida was like, though it does not pretend to have duplicated nature. Upon revisiting it recently, I was struck by its biodiversity, the way the landscape's slope was utilized to create a seemingly natural unfolding of systems — hammock to transition to wetland — offering the essentials for successful wildlife gardening: canopy, cover, food and water. All in a landscape slightly larger than an acre.

Urbanization and agriculture have drastically reduced South Florida's pineland and hardwood hammock ecosystems. The natural areas that remain struggle against an altered water table, vast numbers of exotic plants and the natural destruction wrought by Hurricane Andrew. Pinelands, imperiled and desperately in need of restoration, are a fire-dependent ecosystem requiring periodic controlled burns often impossible in highly urbanized areas. The hammocks — islands of evergreen hardwoods surrounded by differing vegetation — have been just as disturbed, yet they contain many adaptable trees and shrubs that most homeowners can plant and maintain. Wetlands, particularly freshwater marshes, offer a selection of grasses and sedges for landscaping the retention ponds common in suburban developments, while woody plants of swamps are adapted to the water's edge. In other words, the hammock-to-wetland landscape planted by the Forthmans 30 years ago is a combination of habitats that can provide backyard diversity relatively easily.

The Forthmans' property runs from a ridge 15 to 20 feet high down to a 10-acre lake created by a developer. Thirty years ago, there were no handy

A BIODIVERSE GARDEN FOR SOUTH FLORIDA

South Florida's biodiversity was once legendary. The relentless development of recent decades has reduced its pinelands, hardwood hammocks and wetlands to ragged fragments. This plan is based on the garden planted almost 30 years ago by Chirley and Hugh Forthman. It features a seemingly natural unfolding of systems — hammock to a transitional area to wetland — that offers cover, food and water for wildlife, providing backyard diversity relatively easily. Suitable plants for these habitats are listed on the opposite page.

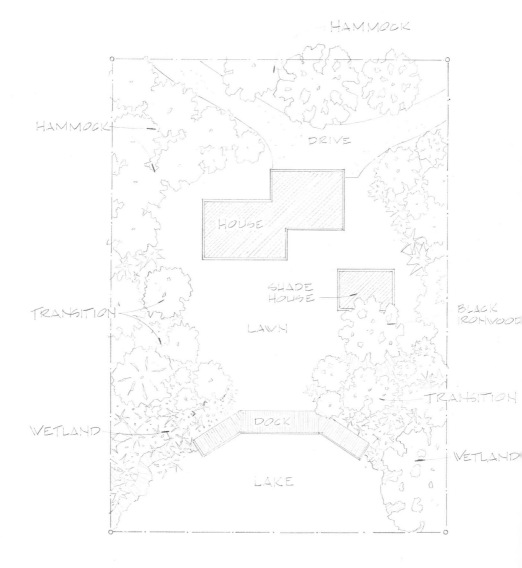

SELECTED NATIVE PLANTS

HAMMOCK:

Jamaica Dogwood *Piscidia piscipula*
Gumbo-limbo *Bursera simaruba*
Pigeon Plum *Coccoloba diversifolia*
Satin-leaf *Chrysophyllum oliviforme*
Paradise Tree *Simarouba glauca*
Willow Bustic *Dipholis salicifolia*
Blolly *Pisonia discolor*
Crabwood *Sapium lucidus*
Wild Tamarind *Lysiloma latisiliqua*
Live Oak *Quercus virginiana*
Black Ironwood *Krugiodendron ferreum*
Shortleaf Fig *Ficus citrifolia*
Bahama Strongback *Bourreria ovata*
Inkwood *Exothea paniculata*
Lignum Vitae *Guaiacum sanctum*
Lancewood *Nectandra coriacea*
West Indian Cherry *Prunus myrtifolia*
West Indian Mahogany *Swietenia mahagoni*
Saw Palmetto *Serenoa repens*
Necklace Pod *Sophora tomentosa*
Simpson Stopper *Myrcianthes fragrans simpsonii*
Spanish Stopper *Eugenia foetida*
Redberry Stopper *E. confusa*
Red Stopper *E. rhombea*
Sumac *Rhus copallina*
Spicewood *Calyptranthes pallens*
Myrsine *Ardisia escallonioides*
Firebush *Hamelia patens*
Tetrazygia *Tetrazygia bicolor*
Wild Coffee *Psychotria* species
Florida Privet *Forestiera segregata*
Ferns *Nephrolepis* species
Cabbage Palm *Sabal palmetto*
Thatch Palm *Thrinax radiata*
Coontie *Zamia pumila*

TRANSITIONAL HABITAT:

Dahoon Holly *Ilex cassine*
Coco Plum *Chrysobalanus icaco*
Buttonwood *Conocarpus erectus*
Redbay *Persea borbonia*
Cabbage Palm *Sabal palmetto*
Wild Lime *Zanthoxylum fagara*
Sweet Bay Magnolia *Magnolia virginiana*
Persimmon *Diospyros virginiana*
Button Bush *Cephalanthus occidentalis*
Wax Myrtle *Myrica cerifera*
Leather Fern *Acrostichum danaeifolium*

WETLAND:

Cypress *Taxodium* species
Redbay *Persea borbonia*
Red Maple *Acer rubrum*
Pond Apple *Annona glabra*
Water Ash *Fraxinus caroliniana*
Paurotis Palm *Acoelorrhaphe wrightii*
Royal Palm *Roystonea* species
Leather Fern *Acrostichum danaeifolium*
Soft Rush *Juncus effusus*
String-lily *Crinum americanum*
Blue Flag Iris *Iris hexagona*
Cordgrass *Spartina* species
Bulrushes *Scirpus* species
Arrowhead *Sagittaria lancifolia*
Pickerel Weed *Pontederia cordata*
Water Lilies *Nymphaea* species
Spatterdock *Nuphar luteum*

guides to landscaping with natives in South Florida, so the Forthmans gathered what information and seeds they could find, spent a lot of time observing how plants grow in the wild and intuited the rest. They cleared their land of invasive exotics. They planted seeds with such enthusiasm they had to rent space at a nearby nursery. That area soon was filled up, so they started their own nursery.

HAMMOCK

A hammock, such as the Forthmans', located relatively close to the Atlantic Ocean, is able to harbor some of the West Indian trees that make their northernmost home in tropical southern Florida and the Florida Keys. Jamaica dogwood, gumbo-limbo and pigeon plum are commonly found in coastal hammocks and are relatively fast-growing. So, too, are the satin-leaf and paradise tree, willow bustic, blolly, crabwood and wild tamarind. The tamarind is one of the first species to colonize disturbed areas, and is especially attractive to small birds as well as tree snails, which browse on the lichens that grow on the bark. Trees can be planted quite close in a home-made hammock; in a natural one they sometimes grow two or three feet apart, with their canopies intertwined. On a northwest corner that will bear the brunt of winter winds, live oak and black ironwood are good choices. Paradise tree, with its glorious new red growth and big leaves, is somewhat brittle and therefore a good species for the middle of the planting, where other, sturdier trees can protect it.

Stoppers, small understory trees, add berries and shelter for birds. The possibilities include Spanish stopper, Simpson or twinberry stopper, redberry and red stopper as well as spicewood. The leaves of the Spanish stopper are small, red when new, and held closely on the slender twigs. Red and redberry have distinct drip-tips. Some choice hammock shrubs are myrsine, with its black fruits eaten by a variety of birds; firebush, with scarlet, tubular-shaped flowers attractive to butterflies and hummingbirds; tetrazygia, for the edges of the hammock where the clusters of white flowers can show off; and wild coffee, with beautiful quilted leaves and red berries. Florida privet makes a good hiding place for little birds. Ferns offer them cover when they forage on nearby open ground. And, of course, the cabbage palm and thatch palm are musts, along with coontie, the little cycad that was close to extinction not long ago.

Bill Harms began converting a tiny urban lot into a natural setting in 1989. The 50-plus plant species are a magnet for butterflies and birds. Florida coontie, a small cycad almost extinct in the wild, grows along the path, opposite the light.

TRANSITIONAL HABITAT

In transitional areas where the hardwood hammock and wetland ecosystems intergrade, dahoon holly makes a pretty statement with its upright crown. The female trees bear bright red fruit in the winter. Coco plum, a big shrub that can take on tree proportions, will go back to the ground in a freeze and so cannot be used too far inland or too far north. Buttonwood, salt tolerant and the most inland member of the mangrove community that fringes South Florida, is tough and durable.

WETLAND

Because wetlands were so central to pre-settlement South Florida, I visited an elaborately restored marsh some 15 miles west of Fort Lauderdale in Tree Tops Park. The marsh simulates conditions that existed before the Everglades drainage canals were built in the early 20th century. Drainage created orange groves and cattle pastures ultimately displaced by urbanization. What had been a low-lying marsh became a haven for opportunistic wax myrtles.

On a fall afternoon, three of us went canoeing there. We tied up our canoe to the boardwalk and identified dog fennel flowering among the willows and spartina blending into the dahoon holly and wax myrtles of the transition zone, then made our way to the laurel oaks, live oaks and cabbage palms on the fringe of the hammock. Some 200,000 new plants have become established.

The ideal way to plant a wetland, say the experts, is to have a slightly sloping shoreline and littoral shelf (that part of the shore that sinks gradually below the water surface and is important habitat for sedges, rushes and grasses). The more irregular the shoreline, the more niches will be available for waterbirds, turtles and other wildlife. Plants should be arranged in zones, beginning at the edge of the water and progressing a few feet into it. It's best to limit the number of aquatics, planting them below the normal water level. Until they become established and fill in, you'll have to weed. Plant soft rush, blue flag iris, cordgrass and bulrush at the upper edge, with cordgrass as the primary plant, interspersed with cannas or iris in clusters for the sheer beauty of it. Plant arrowhead and pickerel weed in the first few inches of water. Water lilies, spatterdock and soft-stem bulrushes complete your home-made wetland, planted to a depth of one to four or five feet.

An egret fishes in a cypress swamp. Gardeners can re-create swamps and freshwater marshes along the retention ponds common in suburban developments.

Southern Live Oak
Quercus virginiana
The matriarch of South Florida trees, growing to 50', with a canopy that's often wider. Provides a picturesque, shady canopy for people and acorns for wildlife. Leathery leaves. Furrowed gray bark provides niches for air plants.

Red Bay
Persea borbonia
Suited to wet sites. A denizen of the Shark River Slough in Everglades National Park as well as the southeast Atlantic coast. Produces small black fruits in late summer. Leaves are aromatic. Provides food for caterpillars of the palamedes swallowtail butterfly.

RED BAY

SOUTHERN LIVE OAK

Bald or Pond Cypress
Taxodium species
Logging operations half a century ago destroyed most of South Florida's cypresses. Feathery deciduous leaves, massive gray trunks with breathing "knees" that rise out of the swamp. Grow in water or upland. New shoots in early spring are as beautiful as anything you've seen. Cones form in early summer.

Firebush

Hamelia patens

Shrub reaching 15' or 20'. A premier butterfly attractor in South Florida's hammocks. Egg-shaped leaves have distinct veins with reddish cast in full sun; in shade, they're plain green. Tubular-shaped red flowers. Cold-tender and can be frozen back to the ground, so use as a background plant.

FIREBUSH

CABBAGE PALM

Wild Coffee

Psychotria nervosa

Beautiful quilted, glossy green leaves and orange to bright red berries in winter make this a choice hammock shrub for humans and wildlife. Flowers begin in spring and can appear all summer. Leaves wilt in response to drought, but the shrub will withstand many soil types.

Necklace Pod

Sophora tomentosa

A coastal shrub with grayish leaves covered with hairs. The pea-like flowers are bright yellow and a source of nectar for hummingbirds. Will take dry conditions in full sun, but gets mold and does not thrive in shade or when overwatered.

Cabbage Palm
Sabal palmetto

Every tropical and subtropical landscape should have a palm or two. This is one of the hardiest. When the fronds fall, the stems break off a few inches from the trunk, forming "boots" that often become homes for ferns or sunning spots for small snakes. Flowers attract bees. Fruits are eaten by a variety of birds.

Leather Fern
Acrostichum danaeifolium

An impressive landscape fern that grows up to 8' tall. Grows in wet conditions at water's edge or in swampy, wet soils. In a lakeside planting, will offer cover for small mammals and birds that forage on or near the ground, such as warblers.

WILD COFFEE

Florida Coontie
Zamia pumila

Small cycad with tough, deep green, prickly leaves growing in a rosette. Nearly pushed to extinction by the early arrowroot starch industry. Still has an uncertain future in the wild but widely grown in nurseries. Food plant of the larvae of the threatened Florida atala butterfly. Plant several clusters.

NECKLACE POD

A JOINT VENTURE WITH NATURE

BY NEIL DIBOLL

IDWESTERN GARDENERS are among the luckiest in the world. Sure, the summers can be brutally hot and dry, the winters fierce and frozen. But these climatic adversities have provided us with some of the toughest native plants around — plants supremely adapted to use in low-care natural landscapes. Best of all, the continental climate of the region favors both prairie and woodland, enabling gardeners to create lush landscapes of tremendous diversity.

PRAIRIE

The quintessential Midwest landscape is the prairie. This vast grassland once stretched from Texas to Manitoba, clothing millions of square miles with a verdant blanket of wildflowers and grasses. One of the most productive ecosystems in the world, the prairie supported an abundance of wildlife, from elk and egrets to bison and butterflies. Today, less than one-tenth of one percent of the Midwest tall-grass prairie remains, making it one of the rarest plant associations in all of North America (the short-grass prairie occurs in the drier Great Plains states to the west). The dense root systems of the prairie plants created some of the finest soils in the world, which were systematically plowed up for agriculture.

DECIDUOUS FOREST

On the perimeter of the prairie, in river valleys, on ridgetops and on lake edges, grow deciduous forests. Closely related to the deciduous woodlands farther east, these Midwest forests feature strong oaks and hickories, fine shade trees such as American ash and sugar maple and berry-producing bird havens like black cherry and hackberry. In the north, stately white pines mingle with the deciduous trees, and in the south, eastern red cedars grow in open areas. Both evergreens provide food and shelter for a variety of birds.

OAK SAVANNA

Between prairie and forest was the oak savanna, where broad oaks and hickories punctuated fields of flowers and grasses. Not surprisingly, the park-like savannas were the first places settled by the pioneers. A variety of shrubs also grew in the savanna, producing valuable nuts and berries for both human and beast — among them wild plums, hazelnuts and elderberries. With this combination of trees, shrubs and grasslands, the savanna offered a diversity of habitats. It is

A BIODIVERSE GARDEN FOR THE MIDWEST

The quintessential landscape of the Midwest is the prairie, which once clothed millions of square miles with a verdant blanket of wildflowers and grasses. Between prairie and forest was the savanna, where oaks and hickories punctuated the grasslands. Today, both prairie and savanna are virtually extinct. This plan replicates the region's lush diversity of landscape types, including a tiny forest north and west of the house, a prairie bisected by a mowed path and a miniature wetland that takes advantage of water runoff from the roof.

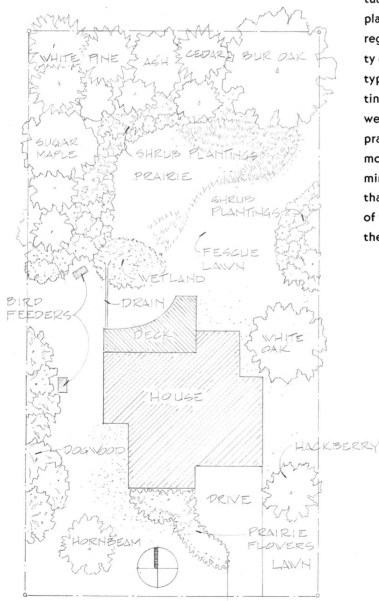

WHITE PINE · ASH · CEDAR · BUR OAK · SUGAR MAPLE · SHRUB PLANTINGS · PRAIRIE · SHRUB PLANTINGS · FESCUE LAWN · WETLAND · BIRD FEEDERS · DRAIN · DECK · WHITE OAK · HOUSE · DOGWOOD · HACKBERRY · DRIVE · HORNBEAM · PRAIRIE FLOWERS · LAWN

SELECTED NATIVE PLANTS

TREES AND SHRUBS:

White Oak *Quercus alba*
Bur Oak *Quercus macrocarpa*
Shagbark Hickory *Carya ovata*
Black Cherry *Prunus serotina*
Hackberry *Celtis occidentalis*
American Beech *Fagus grandifolia*
Sugar Maple *Acer saccharum*
White Ash *Fraxinus americana*
Black Gum *Nyssa sylvatica*
White Pine *Pinus strobus*
Northern White Cedar *Thuja occidentalis*
Eastern Red Cedar *Juniperus virginiana*
Redbud *Cercis canadensis*
Smooth Serviceberry *Amelanchier laevis*
Red-osier Dogwood *Cornus stolonifera*
Nannyberry *Viburnum lentago*
Hazelnut *Corylus americana*
New Jersey Tea *Ceanothus americanus*

WOODLAND WILDFLOWERS:

Columbine *Aquilegia canadensis*
Jack-in-the-pulpit *Arisaema triphyllum*
Wild Ginger *Asarum canadense*
Spring Beauty *Claytonia virginica*
Yellow Lady-slipper *Cypripedium calceolus*
Dutchman's-breeches *Dicentra cucullaria*
Wild Geranium *Geranium maculatum*
Hepatica *Hepatica americana*
Virginia Bluebells *Mertensia virginica*
Wild Blue Phlox *Phlox divaricata*
Mayapple *Podophyllum peltatum*
Jacob's Ladder *Polemonium reptans*
False Solomon's-seal *Smilacina racemosa*
Foamflower *Tiarella cordifolia*
Large-flowered Trillium *Trillium grandiflorum*
Bellwort *Uvularia grandiflora*
Violets *Viola* species

PRAIRIE WILDFLOWERS AND GRASSES:

Little Bluestem *Schizachyrium scoparium*
Sideoats Grama *Bouteloua curtipendula*
Prairie Dropseed *Sporobolus heterolepis*
Indian Grass *Sorghastrum nutans*
Butterfly Weed *Asclepias tuberosa*
Smooth Aster *Aster laevis*
New England Aster *A. novae-angliae*
Pale Purple Coneflower *Echinacea pallida*
Purple Coneflower *E. purpurea*
Rattlesnake-master *Eryngium yuccifolium*
Rocky Mountain Blazingstar *Liatris ligulistylis*
Rough Blazingstar *L. aspera*
Prairie Blazingstar *L. pycnostachya*
Purple Prairie Clover *Petalostemon purpureum*
Yellow Coneflower *Ratibida pinnata*
Sweet Black-eyed Susan *Rudbeckia subtomentosa*
Stiff Goldenrod *Solidago rigida*
Showy Goldenrod *S. speciosa*
Showy Sunflower *Helianthus* x *laetiflorus*
Western Sunflower *H. occidentalis*
Compass Plant *Silphium laciniatum*
Prairie Dock *Silphium terebinthinaceum*
Cup Plant *S. perfoliatum*

WETLAND WILDFLOWERS,
GRASSES & SEDGES:

(for damp soils; standing water in spring only)
Red Milkweed *Asclepias incarnata*
Marsh Marigold *Caltha palustris*
White Turtlehead *Chelone glabra*
Joe-pye Weed *Eupatorium maculatum*
Wild Irises *Iris missouriensis, I. shrevei, I. versicolor*
Queen-of-the-prairie *Filipendula rubra*
Bottle Gentian *Gentiana andrewsii*
Marsh Blazingstar *Liatris spicata*
Turks Cap Lily *Lilium superbum*
Cardinal Flower *Lobelia cardinalis*
Ironweed *Vernonia fasciculata*
Prairie Cordgrass *Spartina pectinata*
Bottlebrush Sedge *Carex comosa*
Porcupine Sedge *Carex hystericina*
Fox Sedge *C. vulpinoidea*

therefore a good model for biodiverse home landscapes that create habitat for both people and wildlife.

WETLAND

The Midwest's mosaic of vegetation types also included valuable wetlands. Marshes, swamps, ponds and lakes dotted the countryside. Wetlands are magnets for birds, reptiles, amphibians and other members of the animal world. They help recharge groundwater supplies while reducing runoff and controlling flooding. With the continuing loss of wetlands to development, the populations of many frogs, turtles, birds and butterflies are dropping precipitously.

A home garden that includes prairie, woodland, savanna and wetland will provide the various habitats that birds, butterflies and other wildlife require at different times of the year. The larval stages of many of the adult butterflies that sip nectar from prairie flowers in summer feed on the leaves of deciduous trees and shrubs in spring. Trees and shrubs provide nesting sites for songbirds, and prairie grasses help camouflage ground-nesting birds such as meadowlarks and bobolinks. In late spring and early summer, the insects produced in the prairie and wetlands are essential food for young birds. In late summer and fall, the nuts and berries of the woodland and savanna as well as the seeds of prairie plants nourish wildlife through the cold winter months. Reptiles and amphibians spend the winter in the mud of wetland ponds.

THE GARDEN PLAN

In the garden plan illustrated on page 38, the various components of the original Midwestern landscape are combined to provide year-round interest and wildlife habitat. Evergreens and deciduous trees are planted on the north and west for privacy, beauty and cover for birds. The protection they afford from winter winds not only benefits birds, but also helps reduce home heating bills. A band of shrubs is planted to the south of the woodland area, easing the transition to the prairie meadow of wildflowers and ornamental native grasses in the full sun to the south. A mowed path bisects the prairie, creating a pleasant walkway while dividing the

Right: A mowed path bisects a prairie planting. This not only allows you to explore your backyard grassland but also divides it into two "management units."

meadow into two "management units." These units should be burned or mowed once a year in alternate years to keep down trees and shrubs and promote vigorous growth of the warmth-loving meadow plants. Only one unit should be burned or mowed at a time so that all the butterfly eggs and chrysalises in your backyard habitat are not destroyed at once. Another trail located between the shrub plantings and the prairie serves as a firebreak and walkway.

A low-maintenance, low-growing and drought-tolerant fescue lawn surrounds the house and extends out to the street. The lawn is punctuated by an occasional tree, just like the oak savanna. The theme of the overall landscape is displayed in the front yard with shrub plantings and a small prairie planting in the front of the house. Shade trees on the southeast side cool the house and driveway during the hot summer months.

A miniature wetland is created using water routed from the roof downspout into the prairie area. Moisture-loving flowers that bloom in late summer are planted here to provide a continuing source of nectar for butterflies and other important insects, as well as seeds for birds in the fall. The land is graded so that excess water is directed into the shrub and woodland area. Miniature wetlands such as this one are easy to construct by utilizing water from roof gutters that might otherwise end up in often overburdened sewage treatment plants. Dig a catchment basin of a few square feet to a depth of one to two feet deep, and plant wildflowers, grasses and sedges that do well in moist soils. Direct rainwater from downspouts via surface or underground drainage hoses to the catchment area. Be sure to make provisions for draining away overflow, so that excess rain won't flood surrounding areas.

Woodland wildflowers can be planted among the trees, once the trees have grown large enough to create a shady canopy, providing blooms in early and mid-spring. In fall the leaves of trees and shrubs take center stage with their flaming reds, yellows and oranges. The tones and textures of tree barks and shrub twigs, along with the gold and bronze prairie grasses, offer winter interest.

It's time to realize that gardening is a joint venture with nature. America, now a Nation of Lawns, can once again become America the Beautiful, with forests, prairies and ponds stretching across the continent. By combining a variety of plants in a number of different habitats, we can have spectacular gardens that are havens for wildflowers, butterflies, birds and the other beautiful creatures that are in danger of disappearing from our land and our lives.

AMERICAN BEAUTIES

Bur Oak
Quercus macrocarpa
A majestic tree with wide-spreading branches and great overall form. Its deeply furrowed black bark is spectacular, especially in winter against snow. Makes a fantastic specimen tree when planted in the middle of a prairie meadow. Its large acorns are a source of winter food for many birds and other animals.

Eastern Red Cedar
Juniperus virginiana
Often overlooked, but a high-quality bird tree for food, cover and nesting. Large specimens may house many nests in a single year. A good choice for southern states where many evergreens cannot tolerate summer heat. Requires full sun. Prefers well-drained, alkaline soils, but will tolerate almost any soil.

Smooth Serviceberry
Amelanchier laevis
Also known as juneberry and shad-blow. The sweet fruits are a favorite summer bird food, and make an excellent pie if you can pick the fruits before the birds do. In fall, foliage turns fiery shades of yellow, gold, orange and red. Grows in moist or dry soils.

EASTERN RED CEDAR

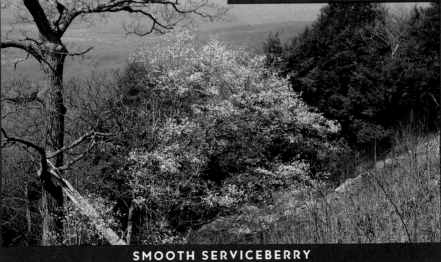

SMOOTH SERVICEBERRY

Red-osier Dogwood
Cornus stolonifera

A top wildlife shrub. Its white berries are a favorite bird food. Goldfinches prefer it for nesting sites. Excellent foliage, large clusters of white flowers in late spring and bright red stems in winter. Grows in full sun in damp soils, but tolerates dry soils. Great for heavy clay. Reaches 4' to 8' tall, forming a patch up to 10' around.

Smooth Aster
Aster laevis

This adaptable, long-lived prairie perennial is covered with bright blue flowers in September. Butterflies appreciate the nectar source late in the season, when few other flowers are available. Foliage has an attractive smooth bluish cast. Grows to a height of 2' to 3'. Does well in almost any well-drained soil.

BUTTERFLY WEED

PRAIRIE BLAZINGSTAR

Prairie Blazingstar
Liatris pycnostachya

One of the most beautiful prairie flowers. The pink wands of this long-lived perennial make a real statement in the summer prairie garden. Prefers rich soils that hold moisture well, such as heavy clay. Good for butterflies and birds.

Butterfly Weed
Asclepias tuberosa
Few other flowers can match this plant's ability to bring in the butterflies! The brilliant orange flowers appear in the heat of mid-summer. Even the pods have their own special beauty in fall. An extremely drought-resistant tap-rooted beauty that can live for decades. Does best when planted among prairie grasses.

Little Bluestem Grass
Schizachyrium scoparium
Bluish-green leaves turn striking reddish bronze in fall, topped with sil-

LITTLE BLUESTEM GRASS

very white seedheads. This heat-loving bunchgrass looks good in all four seasons, and is an important component of the prairie meadow. Grows 2' to 3' tall in any well-drained soil except heavy clay.

Jack-in-the-pulpit
Arisaema triphyllum
This distinctive wildflower's unique bloom becomes even showier when it turns into a cluster of red berries in fall. Grows in dry to damp soils. A number of wild creatures eat the seeds. Often spreads rapidly by seed. One of the best woodland wildflowers.

JACK-IN-THE-PULPIT

WHERE NEATNICKS NEED NOT FEAR TO TREAD

BY C. COLSTON BURRELL

NE OF THE greatest obstacles to wide acceptance of biodiverse gardens in cities and suburbs is the fear of an untidy yard. Neatnick gardeners are quick to point out that their gardens must be well trimmed, staked and carefully constrained. Many people can't stand the thought of a spent flower lingering or — perish the thought — a seedhead left to shatter. Still others fear ecologically sound gardens because they think they'll have to get rid of all their non-native plants.

Conventional gardeners need to be reassured that a biodiverse landscape doesn't have to garner tickets from the weed police. I design many ecologically sound gardens that my urban and suburban clients are happy to live with. Many of these gardens use only plants native to the upper Midwest, but others don't — my own garden, for example.

Designing my garden called for some hard choices. I'm an ardent plant collector, and it was impossible to limit my plant palette to local natives — even here in central Minnesota, where woodland, prairie and oak savanna meet in a kind of ecological crossroads. I garden in the city of Minneapolis, across the Mississippi River from downtown, practically in the shadow of the skyscrapers. My lot is 60 by 150 feet. Some choices were easy. I knew I wanted an ecologically diverse garden in keeping with the natural and cultural history of the upper Midwest, but I wasn't sure what form the garden should take. Despite my predilection to plant a "natural" prairie and be done with it, I observed the garden for a year before I inserted the first trowel. This cooling off period proved to be my smartest move. In time, the simple form of the garden came to me.

The space is dominated by a huge, spreading multi-stemmed box elder. The house and garage sit on the property line, so the garden space is beside and behind the house. This configuration resembles that of many a midwestern farmstead, so I chose a simple axial layout with lush plantings. The inspiration for the plan was the oak savanna, a park-like plant community of prairie plants punctuated by spreading bur oaks with shade-tolerant species growing underneath. I used the trees on my lot as the canopy structure and connected them to the horizontal ground plane with shrubs and herbaceous plants. Woodland plants are placed in the shade of my trees while the open areas become the "prairie." This vertical and horizontal structure recalls the savanna. Neatnicks will note, however, that the garden is still quite formal in layout.

The front walk is bordered by lawn flanked on both sides by beds. The lawn

A BIODIVERSE GARDEN FOR THE CITY

A biodiverse garden doesn't have to garner tickets from the weed police. Cole Burrell's garden, practically in the shadows of Minneapolis's sky-scrapers, is based on a classic axial layout. It includes a small lawn completely enclosed by a perennial border 8 feet deep, shade gardens under the canopies of trees, a prairie planting to the left of the front walk and a bog garden next to the house. Scores of plant species grow in the garden. A diversity of birds, butterflies and other creatures also find refuge on the 1/4-acre lot.

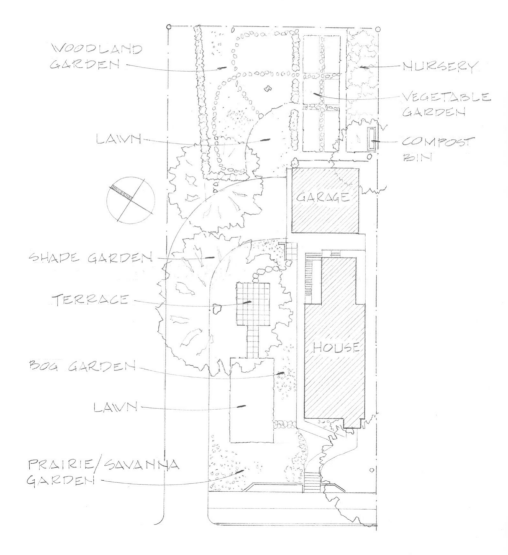

SELECTED NATIVE PLANTS

WOODLAND GARDEN:

White Baneberry *Actaea pachypoda*
Red Baneberry *A. rubra*
Maidenhair Fern *Adiantum pedatum*
Spikenard *Aralia racemosa*
Jack-in-the-pulpit *Arisaema triphyllum*
Wild Ginger *Asarum canadense*
Black Cohosh *Cimicifuga racemosa*
Spring-beauty *Claytonia virginica*
Wild Bleeding-heart *Dicentra eximia*
Squirrel Corn *D. canadensis*
Prairie Shooting-star *Dodecatheon meadia*
Amethyst Shooting-star *D. amethystinum*
Virginia Bluebells *Mertensia virginica*
Wild Geranium *Geranium maculatum*
Cutleaf Toothwort *Dentaria laciniata*
Cow Parsnip *Heracleum lanatum*
Crested Iris *Iris cristata*
Blue Flag *I. versicolor*
Sharp-lobed Hepatica *Hepatica acutiloba*
False Rue Anemone *Isopyrum biternatum*
Twinleaf *Jeffersonia diphylla*
Small Solomon's-seal *Polygonatum biflorum*
Celandine Poppy *Stylophorum diphyllum*
Wild Oats *Uvularia sessilifolia*
Merrybells *U. grandiflora*
Lady Fern *Athyrium filix-femina*
Goldie's Wood Fern *Dryopteris goldiana*
Ostrich Fern *Matteuccia struthiopteris*
Cinnamon Fern *Osmunda cinnamomea*
Interrupted Fern *O. claytoniana*
Northern Beech Fern *Phegopteris connectilis*

DRY SHADE GARDEN:

Wild Columbine *Aquilegia canadensis*
Rue Anemone *Anemonella thalictroides*
Dutchman's-breeches *Dicentra cucullaria*
Wild Sweet William *Phlox divaricata*
Starry Solomon's Plume *Smilacina stellata*
Bloodroot *Sanguinaria canadensis*
Intermediate Wood Fern *Dryopteris intermedia*
Marginal Wood Fern *D. marginalis*
Christmas Fern *Polystichum acrostichoides*
Pennsylvania Sedge *Carex pennsylvanica*

PRAIRIE BORDER:

Anise Hyssop *Agastache foeniculum*
Prairie Onion *Allium stellatum*
Nodding Onion *A. cernuum*
Butterfly Weed *Asclepias tuberosa*
New England Aster *Aster novae-angliae*
Silky Aster *A. sericeus*
Upland White Aster *A. ptarmicoides*
Aromatic Aster *A. oblongifolius*
Smooth Aster *A. laevis*
Dotted Horsemint *Monarda punctata*
Stiff Coreopsis *Coreopsis palmata*
Prairie Clover *Dalea purpurea*
Rattlesnake-master *Eryngium yuccifolium*
Joe-pye Weed *Eupatorium purpureum*
Queen-of-the-prairie *Filipendula rubra*
Prairie Smoke *Geum triflorum*
Prairie Coral Bells *Heuchera richardsonii*
Prairie Blazing Star *Liatris pycnostachya*
Button Liatris *L. aspera*
Dotted Blazing Star *L. punctata*
Penstemons *Penstemon grandiflorus, P. gracilis*
Mountain Mint *Pycnanthemum virginianum.*
Showy Goldenrod *Solidago speciosa*
Prairie Phlox *Phlox pilosa*
Prairie Dock *Silphium terebinthinaceum*
Compass Plant *S. laciniatum*
Pasque Flower *Pulsatilla patens*
Blue-eyed Grass *Sisyrinchium campestre*
Culver's Root *Veronicastrum virginicum*
Prairie Ironweed *Vernonia fasciculata*
Prairie Dropseed *Sporobolus heterolepis*
Switch-grass *Panicum virgatum*
Big Bluestem *Andropogon gerardi*
Little Bluestem *Schizachyrium scoparium*
Sideoats Grama *Bouteloua curtipendula*
Indian Grass *Sorghastrum nutans*

is important as a visual foil for the planting beds as well as to satisfy the neighbors' expectation of my garden. (Most communities have ordinances that prohibit vegetation over a certain arbitrary height, usually 12 inches. The ticketing system is almost always complaint driven, so it is important to appease, as well as educate, your neighbors.) To the right of the lawn is a dry shade garden under a huge hackberry. This garden features drought-tolerant savanna plants such as starry Solomon's plume, sedges and interrupted fern, other natives such as creeping phlox, goatsbeard and crested iris, as well as non-native perennials such as pulmonarias, bergenias and epimediums. Because these plants share the same cultural requirements, they are a viable association.

The main garden consists of a linear sequence of spaces surrounded by planting beds. The front garden receives eight to 12 hours of sun and is planted in an exuberant style reminiscent of the open, "prairie" portion of the savanna. A small lawn 16 by 32 feet is completely enclosed by an herbaceous border eight feet deep. The lawn is a perfect foil for the planting beds and provides a comfortable place for entertaining. In early spring the garden is open to the street, and the wealth of spring bulbs and perennials is enjoyed from inside and out. In July, when the tall prairie plants reach full size, the lawn is quite private. The character of this garden is constantly changing, much the way it is in a native savanna.

The color scheme features purple, blue and white flowers in early summer, with pale yellow used sparingly as an accent. As summer progresses, yellow replaces the blue. Early flowers include prairie phlox, prairie smoke, golden alexanders, columbines, heucheras, daffodils and tulips. Summer flowers include baptisia, coneflowers, mountain mint, garden phlox, beebalm, iris, liatris, silphiums and coreopsis. Late summer and autumn usher in asters, goldenrods, gentians and grasses. The golden and russet stalks are left standing through the winter to provide visual interest, food and cover for wildlife.

An artificial bog was created along the house by excavating an 8 by 25-foot trench two-feet deep. The trench is lined with plastic and filled with rich compost. The bog receives the runoff from the roof and seldom needs additional water. In the bog grow plants that would otherwise require supplemental watering throughout the growing season, including turtleheads, sedges, iris, monkey flower, boneset and vervain, along with non-native ligularias, rodgersias and primroses.

The open lawn leads via a short walkway to a shaded terrace under the box elder. Its branches form a comfortable canopy overhead. Twinflower, wild bleed-

The shade garden in spring, top, and summer, bottom

ing-hearts, crested iris, wild gingers and Solomon's-seal as well as ephemerals such as Virginia bluebell, trout lily, spring beauty and dutchman's-breeches mingle with woodferns and maidenhair. This planting is punctuated by small- to medium-sized shrubs such as winterberry holly, witchhazel and arctic willow.

The back garden area is divided into three sections of roughly equal size — the shade garden, the vegetable garden and the nursery bed. The shade garden is planted under a canopy of aspens and mulberries. The airy canopy and a boundary of hedges gives this garden an intimate feel. It has a complex understory planting of wildflowers, bulbs, ferns and grasses. The planting is modeled on the aspen parkland of the Midwest. This area is the favorite foraging ground of mourning warblers and ovenbirds that routinely stop during their migrations. A hedge of arrowwood viburnum separates the garden from the driveway. The berries are savored by birds in autumn. In summer, catbirds nest in the hedges, and orioles, robins and cardinals devour the ripening mulberries. Last fall, the garden played host to a migrating long-eared owl, and a screech owl often spends the winter there.

The vegetable garden and nursery beds are separated from the shade garden by a low, fine-textured hedge of spiraea. (I use the nursery for propagation as well as for evaluating new plants.) The entire rear garden is held together visually by a low fence festooned with native bittersweet, non-invasive honeysuckles and clematis.

My garden captures the quality of place that makes the upper Midwest look different from other areas of the country. I think the diversity of birds (98 species), butterflies (seven species), bees and other insects and animals (four species) that feed, take refuge and nest in my garden are proof that the design is working ecologically as well.

The shady garden in summer, with the lawn and perennial borders beyond

Flat-topped Aster
Aster umbellatus

Large domed clusters of small, starry white flowers in summer and early fall, followed by tawny seedheads. 3' to 5' tall. Found in prairies and open woods. Plant in moist to wet, average to rich soil in sun or shade. Chickadees and sparrows eat the small fruits. Butterfly larvae feed on the foliage.

prairies, savannas, woodland edges and dry sand plains of the Midwest. Plant in dry to moist, sand or clay soils in full sun or light shade. Space at least 3' apart.

White Turtlehead
Chelone glabra

Erect clumps of leafy stems crowned in late summer by spikes of white flowers, often tinged with purple. Lance-shaped leaves on 2' to 3' stems. Found in low woods, wet meadows and prairies. Requires moist to wet, humus-rich soil in full sun to partial shade.

WHITE TURTLEHEAD

White False Indigo
Baptisia leucantha

A mature clump in full flower is breathtaking. Attains shrub-like proportions. Spikes of dozens of small, pea-like white flowers. Native to

FLAT-TOPPED ASTER

Narrow-leaf Purple Coneflower
Echinacea angustifolia

Our smallest native coneflower, growing 1' to 3' tall on hairy stalks. 2" flowers have short, drooping rays and large, spiny disks. Abounds on the dry prairies of the Great Plains. Thrives on neglect. Grows in dry to moist, average to rich soil in full sun.

Cup Plant
Silphium perfoliatum

A giant among perennials, providing vertical structure and 2 full months of bloom. Grows 6' or more. Paired leaves form a cup around the stem. 3" to 5" flowers in summer and early fall resemble sunflowers. Found in moist to wet prairies and ditches. Need moist to wet, deep soil in full sun or light shade.

ARROW-LEAF PURPLE CONEFLOWER

Quaking Aspen
Populus tremuloides

Beautiful, fast-growing tree. Straight, pale gray trunk. Heart-shaped leaves flutter in the slightest of breezes. Native to oldfields, woodland edges and forest clearings. Plant in moist, average to rich soil in sun or light shade. Grosbeaks, finches and grouse eat the catkins in early spring. Butterfly larvae eat the foliage.

QUAKING ASPEN

PASQUE FLOWER

Pasque Flower

Pulsatilla patens (Anemone patens)

The first flower to open on the prairie in spring. Large, starry, 6-tepaled white to soft blue flowers resemble a fuzzy crocus. Densely hairy leaves deeply divided into narrow segments disappear in summer as soil dries. Native to dry sand or gravel prairies in full sun. Thrives on neglect; plants will rot in good soil.

Stiff Goldenrod

Solidago rigida

Flattened clusters of bright yellow flowers set it apart from other goldenrods. Soft, hairy leaves. Native to prairies, meadows and woodland borders. Plant in dry or moist, average to rich soil in full sun or light shade. Flowers are visited by a variety of nectar- and pollen-feeding insects.

Heart Leaf Golden Alexander

Zizia aptera

Bright yellow flower clusters are harbingers of spring on the prairie. Plants grow 1' to 2' tall. Leaves turn wine-red in autumn. Found in moist to wet prairies, ditches and open woods. Thrive in dry or moist, average to rich soil in sun or shade. Flowers are visited by a variety of nectar- and pollen-feeding insects.

CUP PLANT

55

STRANGER IN A STRANGE LANDSCAPE?

BY SALLY WASOWSKI

VEN THOUGH I was born and raised in Dallas, Texas, I some-times feel like an outsider — for reasons that go way beyond my total indifference to the fortunes of the Cowboys. What makes me feel like I may not belong here are my notions about landscaping; they are clearly out of sync with most of my neighbors.

Folks in these parts think of Big D as the westernmost bastion of the "Old South," where acid soil and rainfall averaging 50 inches a year support southern magnolias, flowering dogwoods, pine trees and azaleas. This attitude does not exhibit a healthy concept of reality. Dallas sits on alkaline clay thinly spread over a base of limestone or shale. Our rainfall averages 35 inches a year, and summer thunderstorms are so scattered that sometimes gardeners don't see a drop from June through September.

Before farmers, ranchers, developers and home gardeners altered the Dallas landscape, it was a lovely mosaic of mid- and tall-grass prairie etched by 30- to 50-foot tall creekside woodlands consisting of an unusual oak-hickory assemblage — shumard oak, chinquapin oak, bur oak, pecan and black walnut. On the exposed limestone bluffs were stunted, 15-foot escarpment woodlands dominated by eastern red cedar and mountain cedar.

The plan for a limestone woodland garden on page 58 shows how our tall and short woodlands blend together. It is a slightly adapted version of my own home garden, which is not entirely native; I've added some naturalized flowers, non-native groundcovers and daffodils, plus an array of plants found in limestone habitats in nearby Arkansas and the Texas Hill Country, but not in Dallas. When we bought our house, we also inherited some plants that are not even native to North America but have withstood our climate without any help. The plant list that accompanies the landscape plan consists only of species found in Dallas, proving that it is also possible to have a handsome garden using a strictly native plant palette.

The garden is divided into three habitats — escarpment, seep and riparian woodland. At the top of the hill is the *escarpment*, the area behind the house where the soil is thin or non-existent over outcrops of soft, yellowish white limestone called Austin chalk. This chalk extends into the upper third of the court-yard until a nine-inch drop in elevation exposes the underlying layer of dark gray Eagle Ford shale. When I leveled a space for the limestone patio, a bit of this juncture was laid open. This is the *seep*, where groundwater oozes between the limestone and shale layers. The *riparian woodland* garden has deep, black clay

A BIODIVERSE GARDEN FOR DALLAS

Most folks think of Dallas as the westernmost bastion of the Old South, where acid soil and plentiful rainfall support magnolias and the like. But the Big D sits on alkaline clay and receives relatively little rainfall. Sally Wasowski based her garden on the original Dallas landscape. In the escarpment, soil, amidst limestone outcrops, is thin. In the seep, groundwater oozes between layers of limestone and shale. The riparian woodland has deep, black soil, once nourished by a nearby creek. The plants opposite are all Dallas natives.

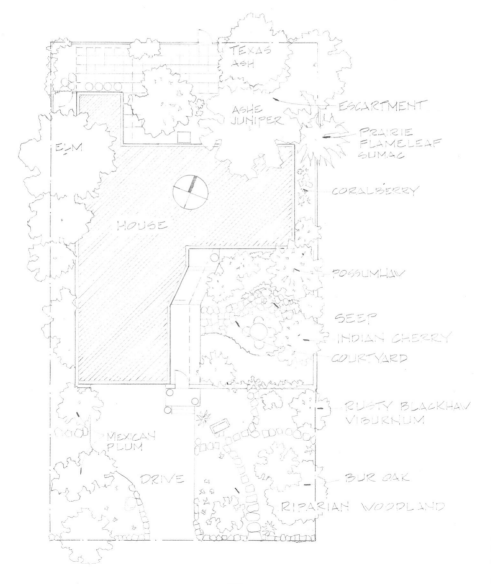

SELECTED NATIVE PLANTS

ESCARPMENT:

(little or no soil over exposed limestone)
Ashe Juniper *Juniperus ashei*
Texas Ash *Fraxinus americana texensis*
Cedar Elm *Ulmus crassifolia*
Shumard Red Oak *Quercus shumardii*
Hackberry *Celtis laevigata*
Prairie Flameleaf Sumac *Rhus lanceolata*
White Honeysuckle *Lonicera albiflora*
Fragrant Sumac *Rhus aromatica*
Coralberry *Symphoricarpos orbiculatus*
Wild Grapes *Vitis cinerea, V. mustangensis*
Snailseed *Cocculus carolinus*
Trout Lily *Erythronium albidum*
Blue-eyed Grass *Sisyrinchium pruinosum*

SEEP:

(more sun and moisture)
Possumhaw *Ilex decidua*
Spring Herald *Forestiera pubescens*
Eastern Red Cedar *Juniperus virginiana*
Trumpet Vine *Campsis radicans*
Indian Cherry *Rhamnus caroliniana*
White Honeysuckle *Lonicera albiflora*
Seep Muhly *Muhlenbergia reverchonii*
Texas Bluebells *Eustoma grandiflorum*
Oak Cliff Spiderwort *Tradescantia occidentalis*
Frogfruit *Lippia incisa*
Wild Ageratum *Eupatorium coelestinum*
Fall Obedient Plant *Physostegia virginiana*
Woodland Silphium *Silphium speciosum*

RIPARIAN WOODLAND:

(deeper soil and dappled shade)
American Elm *Ulmus americana*
Eastern Persimmon *Diospyros virginiana*
Indian Cherry *Rhamnus caroliniana*
Cedar Elm *Ulmus crassifolia*
Roughleaf Dogwood *Cornus drummondii*
Mexican Plum *Prunus mexicana*
Shumard Red Oak *Quercus shumardii*

White Ash *Fraxinus americana*
Dallas Redbud *Cercis canadensis texensis*
Bois D'Arc *Maclura pomifera*
Virginia Wild Rye *Elymus virginicus*
Missouri Violet *Viola missouriensis*
Aromatic Aster *Aster oblongifolius*
Wild Onion *Allium canadense*
Pecan *Carya illinoensis*
Bur Oak *Quercus macrocarpa*
Chinquapin Oak *Q. muehlenbergii*
Rusty Blackhaw Viburnum *Viburnum rufidulum*
Eve's Necklace *Sophora affinis*
Mexican Buckeye *Ungnadia speciosa*
Crossvine *Bignonia capreolata*
American Beautyberry *Callicarpa americana*
Coral Honeysuckle *Lonicera sempervirens*
Inland Sea Oats *Chasmanthium latifolium*
Lyreleaf Sage *Salvia lyrata*
Wild Petunia *Ruellia nudiflora*
Woodland Sedge *Carex blanda*
Blue Spiderwort *Tradescantia ohiensis*
White Avens *Geum canadense*
Green Dragon *Arisaema dracontium*
Meadow Rue *Thalictrum dasycarpum*

RIPARIAN EDGE:

(soil and partial sun)
Aromatic Aster *Aster oblongifolius*
Crow Poison *Nothoscordum bivalve*
Switch-grass *Panicum virgatum*
Winecup *Callirhoe involucrata*
Arkansas Yucca *Yucca arkansana*
Fall Obedient Plant *Physostegia virginiana*
Ironweed *Vernonia baldwinii*
Goldenrods *Solidago* species
Fragrant Phlox *Phlox pilosa*
Winecup *Callirhoe involucrata*
Bergamot *Monarda fistulosa*
White Woodland Boneset *Eupatorium incarnatum*

Limestone woodlands occur along the Appalachians from Kentucky to Texas.

soil and slopes down to the street, dropping about one foot in eight. "Riparian" means close to a river or stream, and our street, which runs nearly a foot deep after a heavy rain, empties into White Rock Lake (previously White Rock Creek) within sight of our house.

ESCARPMENT

The escarpment garden, white with trout lilies and honeysuckle in early spring, is most colorful in the fall. Starting in September, a feast is laid out to tempt migrating birds: grapes, clusters of scarlet honeysuckle, sumac and snailseed berries and coralberries. Over a period of several weeks, ending in December, there is a parade of fall foliage — red from the sumacs and the shumard red oak, orange and mauve from the Texas ash and pure yellow from cedar elm — all set off by the rich evergreen of the ashe junipers.

SEEP

The seep garden is a haven for wildlife in the winter. It provides food and water as well as evergreens for protection from the cold. It also features bright winter color easily seen from the house — the red berries of a possumhaw pruned up like a tree, the blue berries and evergreen foliage of eastern red cedar and the royal purple and green of crossvine and frogfruit. In February spring herald bursts into yellow flowers, sometimes joined by early blossoms of coral honeysuckle and crossvine. Cerisse-colored spiderworts, white honeysuckle, yellow spring silphium, orange trumpet vine, bluebells, bright blue to violet wild ageratum, rose-purple fall obedient plant and the pink mist of seep muhly attract butterflies and hummingbirds from April through October.

RIPARIAN WOODLAND

The riparian garden is lovely in March and April with understory trees abloom in pink or white over pale blue carpets of violets, spiderworts and lyreleaf sage. May finds the garden pink and purple with bergamot and winecup, while summer is blue with ruellia and a rich texture of varying shades of green. The yellow and wine foliage of autumn is accented by grass flowers, American beautyberry, white boneset and asters.

EASY MAINTENANCE

Maintenance is measured in hours per *year*, not hours per week. In early spring, I weed out all the pecans planted by busy squirrels. In late May, I cut back the foliage of early spring flowers and shorten the asters to their bottom four leaves so they'll be three feet, not six feet, by fall. After a killing frost — usually in mid-December — I cut back dead stalks and spread an even comforter of fallen leaves to give winter protection to the roots and to rebuild the soil. If I don't water at all, established plants don't die, but it takes three deep waterings a summer to keep the garden pretty enough to photograph.

I use no pesticides and fungicides. I decided to let nature take its course on the landscape we inherited when we moved into the house. At first I lost a lot of plants, but those that got mauled by pests and dis-

This section of Sally Wasowski's riparian woodland garden gets two hours of sun a day.

eases were those that were already struggling with the soil and climate. I replaced them with natives and now have no problems. We have a growing variety of butterflies and last summer hosted two different kinds of hummingbirds. Lime-green anoles, sometimes miscalled chameleons, sun themselves on the courtyard walls, the males puffing out their luscious pink throats to flirt with the females. We have a plentiful and welcome supply of cicadas, raccoons and opossums, along with a nesting pair each of cardinals, mockingbirds and bluejays. And every spring the waxwings drop by and get snockered on our fermented holly berries.

Limestone gardens have their own character and palette of plants. By following the dictates of soil and climate, it is possible to create a garden that is very low maintenance and also beautiful. Our garden gives Andy and me, as well as our neighbors and many passing bicyclers and joggers, a great deal of pleasure all year. And I get to relax in my garden — not work in it.

Goldenrod blooms in the riparian garden, a sure sign of autumn.

American Beautyberry

Callicarpa americana

Found in both eastern red cedar and pine woodlands. Grows 4' to 8' tall and equally broad with arching branches. Showy clusters of purple berries in fall attract mockingbirds and purple finches, as well as other birds and mammals. Prefers part shade.

Inland Sea Oats

Chasmanthium latifolium

Found in moist thickets and in woodlands along streams. Grows 2'

AMERICAN BEAUTYBERRY

to 5' tall in masses that give the effect of a glade of ferns. Dangling seedheads, ornamental from June to after frost, germinate easily. Prefers dappled shade but will tolerate full sun with water.

Virginia Wild Rye

Elymus virginicus

Found in woodlands and along shaded creeks. Grows 18" to 4' tall. Erect tan spikes of seed feed numerous birds and small mammals from summer to mid-winter. Without water, foliage turns tan in mid-summer, even in deep shade.

INLAND SEA OATS

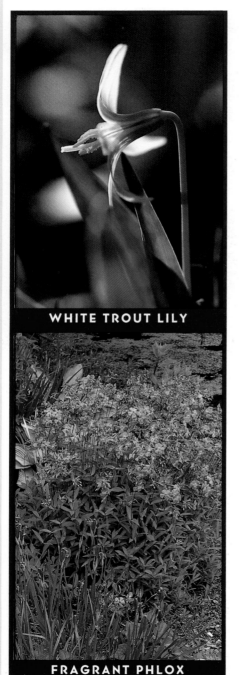

WHITE TROUT LILY

FRAGRANT PHLOX

White Trout Lily (Dog-tooth Violet)

Erythronium albidum

Found in moist or dry woodlands with a thick bed of decomposing leaves. Grows 8" tall. White flowers in early spring. Each flower has one green leaf mottled with purple spots from February to May (dormant rest of year). Seed sown in fall produces flowers the third or fourth spring.

Fragrant Phlox (Prairie Phlox)

Phlox pilosa

Found in sunny prairies and open woodlands and woodland edges. Clump-forming perennial that can grow to 2' tall. Fragrant lavender flowers in April and May, providing nectar for butterflies. Foliage is dormant rest of year. Roots must be mulched to survive the summer.

Wild Petunia

Ruellia nudiflora

Found in woodlands, fields and vacant lots. Grows 10" to 2' high. Scattered blue to lavender flowers from late spring through the hottest part of the summer and on into fall. Flowers attract hummingbirds and butterflies. Tolerates full sun or dappled shade.

Purple Meadow Rue
Thalictrum dasycarpum
Occasionally found here in damp thickets and open woodlands. 4' to 6' when in bloom. Pretty leaves, always green in the winter, go dormant in summer without water. Delicate white flowers in spring.

Blue Spiderwort
Tradescantia ohiensis
Found in prairies and woodland edges. Grows 18" to 30" tall. Grassy blue-green foliage, sometimes dormant in summer and often green in winter. Blue flowers every morning for a long season in spring and again most autumns.

BLUE SPIDERWORT

Missouri Violet
Viola missouriensis
Found in limestone woodlands and along streams. Grows 4" tall and makes mats of green in the winter. Palest lavender to dark purple flowers appear in February. Dappled shade preferred, although morning sun is tolerated. Usually goes dormant in the summer, even if watered.

MISSOURI VIOLET

A LOW-CARE
NATURAL
LANDSCAPE

BY GAYLE WEINSTEIN

COLORADO IS a semi-arid state with minimal precipitation, low humidity, lots of sunshine and generally alkaline soils low in organic matter. These conditions make landscaping in Colorado a challenge, given that most plants used in gardens come from humid areas where soils are richer and neutral to acidic. Most gardeners in this part of the country enrich their soil with amendments and water regularly. This not only wastes precious resources but also turns gardening into a time-consuming chore.

The landscape design plan illustrated on page 68 reflects Colorado's natural beauty. Five of the state's major ecosystems — coniferous forest, pygmy forest, shrubland, short- and mid-grass prairie and riparian wetland — are represented. Because almost all of the plants are native to Colorado and placed in the microclimate that complements their cultural needs, the garden requires a minimum of maintenance.

CONIFEROUS FOREST

On the north boundary of the property is the coniferous forest, where a few mature trees were already in place. Douglas fir, ponderosa pine and Rocky Mountain juniper are the tallest members of this plant community. Common juniper is the primary groundcover. Evergreen needles and pine cones are allowed to accumulate on the forest floor to create a natural mulch. Where there is sunlight, deciduous shrubs such as mountain ninebark, buckbrush and waxflower are planted, adding texture, spring blooms and fall color. For seasonal interest and a more natural look, wildflowers are randomly scattered throughout this forest community, including the native bluebell, which bears delicate, blue, bell-shaped flowers from late spring to mid-summer, and foothills penstemon, with spectacular deep blue to purplish flowers on six- to 12-inch stems in summer. Large boulders are placed in this part of the garden to create the illusion of mountainous terrain.

The coniferous forest provides year-round nesting, food and shelter for a variety of birds, insects and small animals. It's also located on the northwest boundary of the property, where it modifies prevailing winter winds and moderates temperature extremes around the house. The conifers also screen the house from the neighbors and the street.

PYGMY FOREST

Moving eastward along the north property line, the coniferous forest begins to change into a more open, shorter needle evergreen plant community — the

A BIODIVERSE GARDEN FOR COLORADO

T his plan reflects Colorado's natural beauty. Five of the state's major plant communities are represented: coniferous forest, a shorter, more open pygmy forest dominated by pinyon pine and singleseed juniper, shrubland where wildlife flock to thickets of American plum, scrub oak and sumac, mid- and short-grass prairie and riparian (streamside) wetland. Around the house is a low-maintenance lawn consisting of two native grasses — buffalograss and blue grama grass.

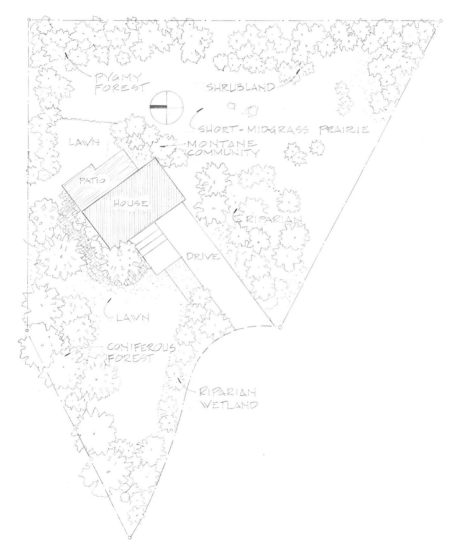

SELECTED NATIVE PLANTS

MID- AND SHORT-GRASS PRAIRIE:

Western Wheatgrass *Agropyron smithii*
Blue Grama *Bouteloua gracilis*
Buffalograss *Buchloe dactyloides*
Junegrass *Koeleria cristata*
Needle and Thread Grass *Stipa comata*
Yarrow *Achillea lanulosa*
Winecup *Callirhoe involucrata*
Indian Paintbrush *Castilleja integra*
Prairie Coneflower *Dalea purpurea*
Wallflower *Erysimum asperum*
Snakeweed *Gutierrezia sarothrae*
Gayfeather *Liatris punctata*
Blue Flax *Linum perenne lewisii*
Tansy Aster *Machaeranthera tanacetifolia*
Evening Primrose *Oenothera lavandulaefolia*
Lambert's Locoweed *Oxytropis lambertii*
Sidebells Penstemon *Penstemon secundiflorus*
Mexican Hat *Ratibida columnifera*
Cowboy's Delight *Sphaeralcea coccinea*
Spiderwort *Tradescantia occidentalis*
Golden Currant *Ribes aureum*
Soapweed *Yucca glauca*

RIPARIAN WETLAND:

Rocky Mountain Maple *Acer glabrum*
Alder *Alnus tenuifolia*
Western River Birch *Betula fontinalis*
Lanceleaf Cottonwood *Populus* x *acuminata*
Rocky Mountain Columbine *Aquilegia caerulea*
Richardson's Geranium *Geranium richardsonii*
Western Blue Flag *Iris missouriensis*
Bluebells *Mertensia ciliata*
Golden Banner *Thermopsis divaricarpa*

PYGMY FOREST:

Big Sagebrush *Artemisia tridentata tridentata*
Rabbitbrush *Chrysothamnus nauseosus*
Snakeweed *Gutierrezia sarothrae*
Singleseed Juniper *Juniperus monosperma*
Pinyon Pine *Pinus edulis*
Indian Ricegrass *Oryzopsis hymenoides*

Western Yarrow *Achillea lanulosa*
Rose Pussytoes *Antennaria rosea*
Indian Paintbrush *Castilleja integra*
Sulphur Flower *Eriogonum umbellatum*
Blanket Flower *Gaillardia pinnatifida*
Skyrocket Gilia *Ipomopsis aggregata*
Evening Primrose *Oenothera caespitosa*
Eaton's Penstemon *Penstemon eatonii*
Cowboy's Delight *Sphaeralcea coccinea*

CONIFEROUS FOREST:

Buckbrush *Ceanothus fendleri*
Waxflower *Jamesia americana*
Common Juniper *Juniperus communis*
Rocky Mountain Juniper *J. scopulorum*
Mountain Ninebark *Physocarpus monogynus*
Ponderosa Pine *Pinus ponderosa*
Douglas Fir *Pseudotsuga menziesii*
Bluebells *Campanula rotundifolia*
Fireweed *Epilobium angustifolium*
Fremont Geranium *Geranium fremontii*
Creeping Hollygrape *Mahonia repens*
Foothills Penstemon *Penstemon virens*

SHRUBLAND:

American Plum *Prunus americana*
Scrub Oak *Quercus gambelii*
Sumac *Rhus glabra cismontana*
Western Wheat *Agropyron smithii*
Sideoats Grama *Bouteloua curtipendula*
Blue Grama *B. gracilis*
Western Yarrow *Achillea lanulosa*
Bluebell Bellflower *Campanula rotundifolia*
James Buckwheat *Eriogonum jamesii*
Wallflower *Erysimum asperum*
Skyrocket Gilia *Ipomopsis aggregata*
Blue Flax *Linum perenne lewisii*
Evening Primrose *Oenothera caespitosa*
Eaton's Penstemon *Penstemon eatonii*
Foothills Penstemon *P. virens*

Short-grass prairie near Mesa, Colorado. The grasses and wildflowers in this plant community are somewhat different from those of the Midwest prairies, where rainfall is more plentiful.

pygmy forest. The dominant plants are pinyon pine and singleseed juniper. Rabbitbrush, snakeweed and big sagebrush offer spring and summer flowers, summer and fall fruit and winter color. Because this area borders a fairly busy street, the trees are arranged in two staggered rows planted densely with the shrubbery amid large boulders. The plants in the pygmy forest are fairly tolerant of salt spray, which can be kicked up off the road during the snowy months. Groundcovers include scattered native grasses and wildflowers such as Indian paintbrush, whose orange to reddish flowers contrast strikingly with the greens, silvers and blues of the woody evergreens. Many plants in this open woodland attract a variety of butterflies, as well as birds such as cedar waxwings and hummingbirds.

SHRUBLAND

On the east property line, the pygmy forest blends into shrubland, where thickets of American plum, scrub oak and sumac prevent pedestrians from cutting across the property. Just west of the thicket is a drainage area planted with wood rose, chokecherry and hawthorn, plants that frequently grow where moisture collects. The fleshy plums, sumac fruits and acorns from the scrub oaks are a magnet for wildlife. Robins, cedar waxwings, tanagers, flickers and butterflies are all drawn to the food these plants provide. Sumacs alone can entice 30 bird species. This area also changes dramatically with the seasons. Plums and roses usher in spring with their fragrant white and pink flowers. Soon, green plums ripen to purple and rose hips turn bright red. The sumac's fall color is unsurpassed.

PRAIRIE

Moving toward the center of the property and the house, the coniferous and pygmy forests and shrubland ease into mid- and short-grass prairie. Filled with

A deer browses in a grassland. Prairies are havens for wildlife. They're unrivaled in producing nectar-bearing plants that attract butterflies. Numerous birds and ground-nesting animals also find their home here.

numerous wildflowers and grasses, this plant community changes in color and texture each season. Buffalograss, blue grama, junegrass, western wheatgrass and needle and thread are the primary grasses. Wildflowers include yarrow, winecup, sundrops, Indian paintbrush, wallflower, blue flax, gayfeather, prairie coneflower and cowboy's delight. A few shrubs, such as soapweed and golden currant, are scattered throughout the prairie.

This grassland community is unrivaled in producing nectar-bearing flowers that attract swallowtails and other butterflies. Numerous insects and ground-nesting animals also find their home here, including lark buntings and meadowlarks.

RIPARIAN WETLAND

On either side of the driveway is the riparian (streamside) wetland community. Because this area is designed to collect irrigation and stormwater runoff, the planting needs little supplemental water. Lanceleaf cottonwoods are the large trees here. The smaller trees and shrubs include Rocky Mountain maple, western river birch, thinleaf alder, bluestem willow and red-osier dogwood. The riparian wetland not only helps moderate summer heat but also provides an array of red, white and silver stem colors in winter. What's more, it meets the basic needs of wildlife: food, water, cover and nesting sites.

Two other types of plantings complete the garden. Surrounding the house is a lawn comprising two native grass species — buffalograss and blue grama, which replace a Kentucky bluegrass lawn that required weekly watering. By contrast, the native dryland lawn may require irrigation once every three weeks if there is little or no natural precipitation. It is fertilized once, in late spring, and mowed just three to six times during the growing season.

A montane community found at higher elevations screens the bedroom from the patio. Quaking aspens provide an airy screen. The trees' shimmering leaves are lovely by day, and their peaceful rustling sound is very soothing in late evening. Wildflowers, including blue and white columbines and bright-yellow golden banner, take advantage of the cool filtered shade cast by the aspens. This area has rich, organic soil and receives additional moisture from the rainwater harvested from roof downspouts. Here, as well as in the wetland planting, drip irrigation provides supplemental irrigation when soil moisture is not replenished by natural precipitation.

Rabbitbrush

Chrysothamnus nauseosus

Grows between 3,000' and 8,000' in dry grasslands, open woodlands and gullies. Needs very little water. Leaves are green to silvery blue; stems woolly white. Has a mounded growth habit, growing 1' to 6' high with a 1' to 2' foot spread. Outstanding sulfur yellow flowers in late summer attract butterflies.

RABBITBRUSH

GOLDEN CURRANT

Golden Currant

Ribes aureum

Deciduous shrub found along streambanks and moist canyon bottoms. Erect, loosely branched, 5' to 6' high and 4' to 5' wide. Foliage turns fiery tones in fall. Yellow spring flowers have a spicy fragrance. Fruits are wildlife favorites. Needs little water. Adaptable to most soils.

Big Sagebrush

Artemisia tridentata tridentata

Native to the intermountain grasslands and mountain slopes from 1,500 to 10,600 feet. Evergreen, silvery gray shrub 3' to 8' tall and 4' to 6' wide. Needs well-drained soil, little water. Picturesque, stiff, upright, irregular growth habit. A good browse and nesting plant for wildlife.

ROCKY MOUNTAIN MAPLE

Rocky Mountain Maple

Acer glabrum

Deciduous, shrub-like tree found along streams and lakeshores. Can reach 20' to 30' tall and 15' wide. Yellow fall color. Outstanding upright form with silver gray bark and contrasting red buds in winter. Prefers moist, well-drained, rich soil and moderately sunny sites. Performs poorly in alkaline heavy soils.

Creeping Hollygrape

Mahonia repens

Broadleaf evergreen shrub found in mountainous areas. Grows in sun or shade in sandy, chalky or rocky soils. Needs little water. An excellent groundcover 1' to 2' high. Bluish green foliage turns reddish in winter. Sweetly fragrant yellow flowers in spring, followed by clusters of purplish grape-like fruits.

Waxflower

Jamesia americana

Deciduous shrub found in forests and canyons and along streamsides. 4' to 5' tall and wide. Many ornamental features: brown peeling bark, foliage that turns red to orange in fall, clusters of white to pale pink waxy flowers in spring. Prefers full sun or partial shade in well-drained soil.

PENSTEMON

BUCKWHEAT

cream, white, yellow and pink are attractive in groups. Prefer well-drained soil and full sun. Deep tap roots make them very drought tolerant but difficult to move around.

Evening Primrose
Oenothera species
Intriguing wildflowers for natural landscapes in the West. Many species found in desert areas with less than 8" of annual precipitation; others in canyons and mountainous habitats with 15" of precipitation. Vary in form and habit. Require full sun in well-drained soil.

Penstemons
Penstemon species
Many native species, found at most elevations in a variety of habitats. Spike-like flowers range in color from red to blue to white to yellow. Adaptable to most soils but will not tolerate standing water or poorly aerated soil. Use in grassland, woodland or forest plantings or traditional flower borders and rock gardens.

Buckwheats
Eriogonum species
Among the most versatile plants for natural gardens. Most of the 200 or so known species are native to the western states. Small flowers in

EVENING PRIMROSE

BIODIVERSITY
IN THE
DESERT

BY CAROL SHULER

DECEMBER IS ALREADY HERE. It's autumn, winter in the rest of the country. We had a nice rain, over two inches, in early October. The rain brought winter grasses into luxuriant growth. Shrubs that were dried up or leafless in summer now sport a new flush of foliage. Many of the spring wildflowers have germinated. If we don't get more rain this winter, it will be another poor year for wildflowers.

I am a landscape architect. My husband is a botanist. We're both plant collectors. His special expertise is cacti and succulents. I'm interested in any plant adapted to our local conditions. Our home is located in the Sonoran Desert on the northern fringe of Phoenix, Arizona. It is our laboratory.

The house was placed on the 1-1/4-acre site with minimal disturbance to existing native vegetation. The major plants on the site are foothill palo verde, creosote bush, desert hackberry, saguaro, buckhorn cholla and compass barrel. Bursage, a tough little gray-green shrub, forms a dense groundcover in the driest areas. Various annual wildflowers come and go with the seasons — or don't show up at all, depending on conditions. Washes crisscross the site. Most of them carry water only for a few hours during thunderstorms.

Our climate is one of extremes, yet subtle differences in conditions have a great impact. While summer daytime temperatures can be scorching, nighttime lows are comparatively chilly — a 30- to 40-degree temperature swing from day to night is common. In winter, hard frosts occur frequently enough to prohibit growing tropical plants in all but the most protected spots. Long droughts and occasional floods are a natural part of our weather pattern. The 12 inches of precipitation that we receive on average every year comes from gentle winter rains and violent summer storms. Gardening is difficult in this climate. But by selecting plants native to the Sonoran Desert and other arid habitats, you can have great success with minimal effort.

Maintaining the indigenous character of our property is important to us. We're working to not only preserve but also enhance the several wildlife habitats on the site: desert xeric riparian, which occurs along the washes, interwash zone and mesquite bosque. The densest and most diverse native vegetation grows astride the washes. The larger trees and shrubs provide shade and protect the more delicate species from frost. The vegetation serves as a living mulch, cooling the soil and reducing evaporation. A myriad of wildlife, from insects to sizable mammals such as bobcats and javalina, depends on this habitat for food and

A BIODIVERSE GARDEN FOR ARIZONA

Maintaining the indigenous character of their desert property is very important to Carol Shuler and her husband, a botanist. They're working to not only preserve but also enhance several wildlife habitats on the land. The densest and lushest native vegetation grows astride the washes that crisscross the site. The house and traditional plantings are confined to the interwash zones, the driest areas of the desert. Mesquite trees, native grasses and wildflowers grow in the bosque, a low, flat area in the floodplain of a wash.

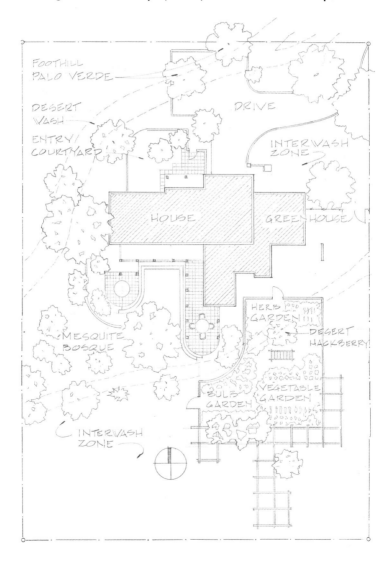

SELECTED NATIVE PLANTS

DESERT WASH:

Foothill Palo Verde *Cercidium microphyllum*

Velvet Mesquite *Prosopis velutina*

Catclaw Acacia *Acacia greggii*

Desert Hackberry *Celtis reticulata*

Saguaro *Carnegiea gigantea*

Chuparosa *Justicia californica*

Comatilla *Ephedra trifurca*

Ironwood *Olneya tesota*

Wolfberry *Lycium fremontii*

Banana Yucca *Yucca baccata*

Purple Three-awn *Aristida purpurea*

INTERWASH ZONE:

Saguaro *Carnegiea gigantea*

Buckthorn Cholla *Opuntia acanthocarpa*

Compass Barrel *Ferocactus acanthodes*

Strawberry Hedgehog *Echinocereus engelmannii*

Fishhook Cactus *Mammillaria microcarpa*

Desert Christmas Cactus *Opuntia leptocaulis*

Engelmann Prickly Pear *Opuntia engelmannii*

Bursage *Ambrosia deltoidea*

Ocotillo *Fouquieria splendens*

Jojoba *Simmondsia chinensis*

Creosote Bush *Larrea divaricata*

Desert Lavender *Hyptis emoryi*

Penstemons *Penstemon parryi, P. eatonii, P. spectabilis, P.pseudospectabilis, P. subulatus*

MESQUITE BOSQUE:

Velvet Mesquite *Prosopis velutina*

Muhlenbergia *Muhlenbergia capillaris, M. dumosa, M. emersleyi, M. lindheimeri*

Purple Three-awn *Aristida purpurea*

Alkali Sacaton *Sporobolus airoides*

Colorado Four-o'clock *Mirabilis multiflora*

Sweet Four-o'clock *M. longiflora*

Aster *Aster spinosus*

Spreading Fleabane *Erigeron divergens*

shelter. Because washes are havens for plants and wildlife and are also prone to flash floods during the rainy season, it's important not to build on them. Urbanization of the desert has had the greatest impact on this habitat.

Interwash zones are the driest areas of the desert, as the rain that falls on them drains into adjacent washes. Trees are scattered and smaller than those along the washes. Creosote is the most common large shrub; bursage, the dominant groundcover. A variety of cacti populate interwash areas.

Mesquite bosque, a comparatively rare habitat, is found in low, flat areas in the floodplains of washes or rivers. Mesquite crowd together, forming a dense canopy. In the shade underneath grow native grasses and a few wildflowers.

DESERT WASH

A small, well-defined wash crosses the front of our property. Several foothill palo verde congregate along it. A pair of juvenile saguaro push up through one of the trees. In open areas along the banks of the wash we've added three palo brea, a tree native to the central Sonoran Desert, Mexico and Baja California with a distinctive angular growth habit. Planted under the protection of the new trees are a variety of native penstemons, including the canyon penstemon. In spring, stalks of large fuchsia flowers rise above its rounded, dark-green, serrated leaves. Sev-

The Sonoran Desert is a land of extremes of temperature and precipitation. In desert gardens it makes sense to use plants naturally adapted to such conditions.

In Carol Shuler's garden, low walls separate traditional plantings from the natural landscape. The native *Muhlenbergia lindheimeri* arches gracefully behind the wall.

eral species of aloe from Africa also grow beneath the palo brea. Hummingbirds love both the aloes and the penstemons. Orioles and gila woodpeckers sip nectar from the tall-stemmed aloes. Two native shrubs have also been added: desert lavender, which was used by pioneers as potpourri, and chuparosa, with bright-red flowers that bloom in early spring and are relished by hummingbirds.

INTERWASH ZONE

Construction of our home was confined to the interwash habitat to minimize impact on the natural drainage patterns on the site. Walls screen our outdoor living areas from the neighbors. Inside the walls, the goal was to create rich tapestries that feature the wonderful colors and textures of arid-region plants from around the world.

The entry courtyard is planted as a cottage garden with a grove of *Acacia berlandieri,* commonly known as guajillo, a small tree with lush, lacy foliage native to the Chihuahuan Desert in Texas and Mexico. Among the trees grow flowering shrubs and drought-tolerant perennials. One of the many birds that forage in the courtyard is the precocious cactus wren. It looks for larvae of the sphinx moth under the leaves of the white evening primrose. When it finds a larva, the wren carries it to the top of the courtyard wall and tenderizes it with a few whacks before gulping it down. Many butterflies also congregate here — at least six species can be observed on a summer day.

Plants with higher water requirements and those less tolerant of the heat are placed close to the house's north-facing wall. These include old-fashioned hollyhocks from an old mining town and a prolific small-flowered coneflower from the Northeast. Several plants native to riparian canyons at a slightly higher elevation grow in this microclimate, including coral-flowered scarlet betony *(Stachys coccinea)*, the beautiful golden-flowered columbine, *Aquilegia chrysantha*, and the red-flowered honeysuckle, *Lonicera sempervirens,* which fills a shady corner. Hummingbirds flock to all these plants.

In the backyard, two gently curving walls separate outdoor living areas from the natural landscape beyond. Steps leading from the patio down to the natural grade showcase part of our large, potted cactus and succulent collection. At least one species is blooming nearly every day of the year.

Behind the eastern wall are an herb garden, vegetable garden and bulb garden, protected from critters with a chicken-wire fence. Gates are constructed of saguaro ribs. Quail and other birds roost in the native desert hackberry in the herb garden. Many unusual herbs with long ethnobotanical histories are planted in this garden, including Mt. Atlas anise, which makes a delicious sun tea used by the Tarahamarra Indians of the Sierra Madre. In the vegetable garden we grow many Native American crops offered by Native Seed Search in Tucson. They are exceptional performers in our climate. Our absolute favorite is the yellow-meated pima watermelon.

MESQUITE BOSQUE

Southwest of the spa is our little bosque, which consisted of one native mesquite and exotic annual grasses. We've added nursery-grown mesquite and native perennial bunchgrasses. The grasses include various species of *Muhlenbergia,* which grow an impressive three to four feet high, *Aristida purpurea*, with seedheads that shimmer in the breeze, and *Sporobolus airoides*, which once was common in the area but was destroyed by overgrazing. For color we've added an unusual yellow-flowered chuparosa and desert bird of paradise, *Caesalpinia gilliesii,* an Argentine native that has naturalized throughout the Southwest.

Nestled in the bosque is a triangular shade canopy constructed of recycled corrugated steel roofing. One side rests on a free-standing wall. Supporting the remaining corner is steel pipe column around which multistrand steel cables are entwined in a vine-like pattern, which was designed by a local artist. The shelter is a great place to get away from it all or observe wildlife.

AMERICAN BEAUTIES

Buckhorn Cholla
Opuntia acanthocarpa

Covers large areas of the Sonoran Desert. Flower color varies from yellow to orange to rose. Matures at 3' to 5' in height. Before transplanting or pruning, dampen with a gentle spray of water to keep the small, splinter-like spines, called glochids, from blowing around.

Creosote Bush
Larrea divaricata

The most common shrub in all the American deserts but underused in gardens. Graceful branch structure. Small, bright olive-green leaves. Showy yellow flowers in the warm season after rainfall, followed by furry white fruit. Emits a wonderful fragrance after it rains. Grows 4' to 8' high. Space 6' to 8' apart.

Saguaro
Carnegiea gigantea

The largest cactus in the American deserts. Native only to the Sonoran Desert. May live 250 years and grow to 40' tall with many "arms." White flowers in May are pollinated by bats, moths and birds. The fruit, which ripens in July, is another bonus for wildlife. Birds from hawks to woodpeckers nest in the cactus.

SAGUARO

BUCKHORN CHOLLA

Velvet Mesquite
Prosopis velutina

One of the hardiest and most useful native trees. Gray-green leaves and rough dark bark. Creamy flowers in spring beloved by bees. Grows 20' to 30' tall. Plant at least 20' apart. Limited nursery stock, but salvaged specimens are available. They're costly, but the immediate sculptural effect is worth the price.

PENSTEMON

Compass Barrel
Ferocactus acanthodes

Tips to the south or southwest, giving the cactus its common name. Skin is dark green, spines rose-red to yellow. Yellow-orange flowers appear April to June. Grows 2' to 4' tall. Space 2' to 4' apart. Very cold- and drought-tolerant. Protected by state law. Buy only plants with Arizona Department of Agriculture tags.

Penstemons
Penstemon species

Beautiful wildflowers with sparse, low-growing foliage 1' to 3' high. Tall, 2' to 6' stalks with red, pink, purple, blue or white blooms in spring and summer. Hummingbirds can't resist the flowers. Plant 2' to 3' apart in well-drained soil. Provide afternoon shade in the desert. Don't over-water during summer.

Chuparosa
Justicia californica

Blue-green stems and leaves. Showy red-orange tubular flowers beloved by hummingbirds from February to May and again in the fall. Flowers have a cucumber flavor and can be used in salads. Grows 4' to 6' high. Plant 6' apart. Usually found along washes and needs supplemental water in the garden.

Purple Three-awn
Aristida purpurea

Native perennial bunchgrass about 16" tall. Very drought-tolerant. Early spring blooms are an attractive burgundy color. Shimmers like wheat in the breeze.

Foothill Palo Verde
Cercidium microphyllum

The toughest palo verde in the Arizona desert. Grows 20' tall with a 20' spread. Foliage and bark are lime-green. Flowers are soft, sulfur yellow. Grows slowly, so few nurseries propagate foothill palo verde, but boxed specimens rescued from the path of development are available.

PURPLE THREE-AWN

CHUPAROSA

A GARDEN THAT REDEFINES OUR ROLE IN NATURE

by Ron Lutsko, Jr. and Robyn S. Menigoz

T FIRST GLANCE, a biodiverse garden would seem to be one that re-creates the natural landscape. But what is the "natural landscape?" The term has come to mean land untouched by human hands. The truth is that human beings are as "natural" as any other living creature; we simply have a disproportionately large influence on the environment. So a biodiverse garden should not simply replicate wild settings but rather re-define the relationship between people and the rest of nature in a more sensitive way.

An ecological landscape design should achieve a number of goals. It should not waste water and other resources. It should preserve the diversity of local plant life, and preserve or replace habitat that supports local animal life. The aesthetic goals are harder to define. We strive to create beautiful, comfortable and inspirational gardens that encourage an appreciation of the natural settings in which we live. We also try to make our gardens educational, because when people have a deeper understanding of the environment they become more concerned about their impact on it. What's more, a garden should tell a story about the relationship between humans and the larger natural world.

The landscape illustrated in the plan on page 88 is the Lindsay Natural History Museum garden. Although it is a public garden, the one-acre site is residential in scale and located in a neighborhood in Walnut Creek, California, in a foothill valley 25 miles east of San Francisco.

The landscape comprises several gardens within the garden. For educational purposes we created a nectar garden for butterflies and hummingbirds and a demonstration garden of drought-tolerant plants. Several local plant communities are represented in the redwood grove, the oak woodland, the bunchgrass meadow and the chaparral garden. Planted largely with native plants, they contribute to genetic diversity and create wildlife habitat.

Three gardens directly address the relationship between humans and the rest of nature. The formal entry garden celebrates gardens created specifically for people. Aside from a small arc of lawn, all plants are drought-tolerant natives, proving that people can create a landscape with only their own needs in mind yet still be ecologically responsible. The oak woodland, which at first appears naturalistic, on closer examination reveals itself to be a garden based on an agricultural grid, with oaks, grasses and iris planted like row crops. This garden also

A BIODIVERSE GARDEN FOR THE CALIFORNIA FOOTHILLS

lthough this is the Lindsay Natural History Museum garden, the one-acre site is residential in scale and located in a neighborhood in a foothill valley east of San Francisco. Several local plant communities are represented in the redwood grove, oak woodland, chaparral garden and bunchgrass meadow, a habitat that once covered vast expanses of the state. The demonstration garden of drought-tolerant plants and the nectar garden for butterflies and hummingbirds are also easily adapted for backyard use.

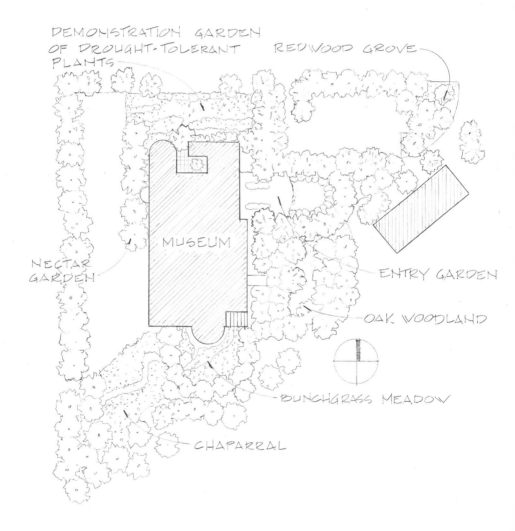

DEMONSTRATION GARDEN OF DROUGHT-TOLERANT PLANTS

REDWOOD GROVE

MUSEUM

NECTAR GARDEN

ENTRY GARDEN

OAK WOODLAND

BUNCHGRASS MEADOW

CHAPARRAL

SELECTED NATIVE PLANTS

ENTRY GARDEN:

California Black Oak *Quercus kelloggii*
Valley Oak *Q. lobata*
Vine Maple *Acer circinatum*
Bush Anemone *Carpenteria californica*
Snowdrop Bush *Styrax officinalis californicus*
Baker's Manzanita *Arctostaphylos bakeri* 'Louis Edmunds'
Wild Lilac *Ceanothus thyrsiflorus* 'Skylark'
Leafy Reed Grass *Calamagrostis foliosa*
Torrent Sedge *Carex nudata*
Douglas Iris *Iris douglasiana* 'Canyon Snow'
Tiger Lily *Lilium pardalinum*

OAK WOODLAND:

Valley Oak *Quercus lobata*
Western Hazelnut *Corylus cornuta californica*
Coffeeberry *Rhamnus californica* 'Eve Case'
Monterey Manzanita *Arctostaphylos hookeri* 'Wayside'
Toyon *Heteromeles arbutifolia*
Currant *Ribes sanguineum glutinosum*
Leafy Reed Grass *Calamagrostis foliosa*
Purple Needlegrass *Stipa pulchra*
Ithuriel's Spear *Triteleia laxa*
Dutchman's Pipe Vine *Aristolochia californica*

BUNCHGRASS MEADOW:

Foothill Pine *Pinus sabiniana*
Buckeye *Aesculus californica*
Wild Lilac *Ceanothus* 'Concha'
Baker's Manzanita *Arctostaphylos bakeri* 'Louis Edmunds'
Vine Hill Manzanita *A. densiflora* 'Sentinel'
Needlegrass *Stipa* species
Tufted Hair Grass *Deschampsia caespitosa*
California Fescue *Festuca californica*
Deer Grass *Muhlenbergia rigens*
Mule's Ear *Wyethia mollis*

Checkerbloom *Sidalcea malviflora*
Baby Blue Eyes *Nemophila menziesii*
Chinese Houses *Collinsia heterophylla*
Farewell to Spring *Clarkia amoena*
Goldfields *Lasthenia chrysostoma*
Lupine *Lupinus nanus*

CHAPARRAL GARDEN:

Baker's Manzanita *Arctostaphylos bakeri* 'Louis Edmunds'
Wild Lilac *Ceanothus* 'Concha'
Jim Sage *Salvia clevelandii*

REDWOOD FOREST:

Redwood *Sequoia sempervirens*
Evergreen Huckleberry *Vaccinium ovatum*
Coffeeberry *Rhamnus californica* 'Eve Case'
Wild Ginger *Asarum caudatum*
Douglas Iris *Iris douglasiana* 'Canyon Snow'
Inside-out Flower *Vancouveria hexandra*
Western Sword Fern *Polystichum munitum*

NECTAR GARDEN:

Fuchsia-flowering Gooseberry *Ribes speciosum*
Coral Bells *Heuchera* species

DEMONSTRATION GARDEN:

Pink Winter Currant *Ribes sanguineum* 'Pulsborough Scarlet'
Wild Lilac *Ceanothus thyrsiflorus* 'Skylark'
Manzanita *Arctostaphylos* 'Pacific Mist'
California Fuchsia *Zauschneria californica*

duplicates the multi-layered architecture of wild woodlands. Here the message is that it is possible to have agriculture that retains wildlife corridors and utilizes crops suited to the natural ecology of a region. The native bunchgrass meadow portrays the California landscape in its purest form, before European settlement. This habitat once covered vast expanses of the state. Today, it survives only in isolated, endangered fragments.

The plant communities are represented, not replicated in detail as is done in ecological restoration work. Representative plants from each community were selected for their beauty, ability to perform in a garden situation, cultural interest and importance to wildlife. Because they duplicate the architecture of the various plant communities, the gardens are diverse in a biological sense; each vegetation layer provides forage or cover for different species of wildlife.

ENTRY GARDEN

An allée of California black oaks lines the entry walk to the museum. Planted beneath the trees are bush anemone, snowdrop bush, mock orange (*Philadelphus* 'Belle Etoile') and perennials, including Douglas iris and tiger lily. Vines such as wild grape climb the building and drape gracefully from trellises. In the courtyard at the main entrance, stately valley oaks stand like columns. Underneath grow leafy reed grass and Douglas iris.

OAK WOODLAND

Valley oaks comprise the canopy of the oak woodland. Dutchman's pipe vine is trained up the oaks. The shrub layer consists of the native hazelnut, coffeeberry, Monterey manzanita, toyon and currant. Leafy reed grass, California needle grass and Ithuriel's spear make up the herbaceous layer. Each of these plants provides something for wildlife, from butterflies to opossums.

BUNCHGRASS MEADOW

Foothill pines define the outer edge of the meadow along with wild lilac and Baker's manzanita. Buckeye and Vine Hill manzanita are planted next to the path to give the garden a more intimate feel. Native bunchgrasses accentuated with Ithuriel's spear, mule's ear, with its soft gray leaves and yellow daisy flowers, hollyhock-like checkerbloom, with spikes of pink cup-shaped flowers, and a mix of native annuals combine to create a tapestry of the finest threads.

California's wild lilac, *Ceanothus thyrsiflorus*, is a spectacular garden plant.

CHAPARRAL

Chaparral is a dense thicket of shrubs native to sunny, dry, exposed hillsides. The museum's chaparral garden is a flowering profusion of Baker's manzanita, with its drooping clusters of urn-shaped flowers, wild lilac, with its deep-blue blooms, and *Salvia clevelandii*, which bears candelabrate spikes of electric lavender-blue flowers. These shrubs provide food and shady shelter for beneficial insects, birds and small mammals.

REDWOOD FOREST

Below the main parking lot is the redwood forest. Redwoods tower over two kinds of shrubs, huckleberry and coffeeberry. Growing in the shade cast by the giant trees, wild ginger, Douglas iris, western sword fern and inside-out flower offer food for insects and birds and damp cover for amphibians.

NECTAR GARDEN

Among the colorful entrées in the nectar buffet designed for butterflies and hummingbirds at the entrance to the museum's wildlife hospital are two persimmon trees, fuchsia-flowered currant, *Penstemon* 'Firebird', with spikes of red, tubular flowers, and flowering oregano (*Origanum laevigatum* 'Hopley's Variety'), a mounding perennial that becomes a haze of small purple blooms all summer long. Sages, coral bells, lavenders, sunflowers, fleabanes and meadow rues complete the feast.

DEMONSTRATION GARDEN

This garden, which faces the street, combines native and exotic plants that are drought tolerant, low maintenance and colorful, and supply food for beneficial insects and birds. Non-natives include rosemary, santolina, euphorbia and sage. Among the notable natives are wild lilac and California fuchsia. For more on these plants, see "American Beauties," page 93.

With some 5,090 species of higher plants, California is by far the most diverse state. Individual species and entire plant communities are threatened by development. West of the Sierras, native oak woodlands, grasslands and chaparral have been drastically reduced by development.

CALIFORNIA FUCHSIA

California Black Oak
Quercus kelloggii

Majestic drought-tolerant tree with large, lobed leaves. Beautiful pink new growth and gold-green catkins. The black bark of mature specimens gives this tree its name. Brilliant fall color. An important plant for butterflies, arboreal salamander, western toad, gray squirrel and a variety of birds.

Bush Anemone
Carpenteria californica

Shrub with lush green leaves. Grows to 6' by 6'. Large, saucer-shaped, fragrant white flowers in May and June. A rarity in California's Sierra foothills in streamside, chaparral and oak woodland habitats. Attracts bees and other beneficial insects. Prefers part shade, occasional water.

California Fuchsia
Zauschneria californica

Perennial with silver mounds of fine-textured foliage. Showy, trumpet-shaped, scarlet flowers in late summer and fall are pollinated by bees (who are too fat to fit in the flowers, but they've learned to poke a hole in the bloom to get the nectar) and hummingbirds. Needs full sun, good drainage. Drought-tolerant.

CALIFORNIA BLACK OAK

DOUGLAS IRIS

Douglas Iris
Iris douglasiana 'Canyon Snow'
Large white flowers with a yellow blotch from March to May. Blue-green, bladed, evergreen foliage in dense clumps. Native from central western California to southwestern Oregon in grasslands, especially near the coast. Prefers part shade in the interior, full sun on the coast. Needs little or no water.

DUTCHMAN'S PIPE VINE

Baker's Manzanita
Arctostaphylos bakerii
'Louis Edmunds'
Vase-shaped, upright growth habit. Deep pink flowers in late winter. Hummingbirds love the flowers. Various birds and omnivores feed on the berries, which look like pippin apples the size of large peas. Requires hot sun, well-drained soil, little water.

Dutchman's Pipe Vine
Aristolochia californica
A well-branched vine with intriguing "curved pipe" blooms and heart-shaped leaves. Important host plant for the pipevine swallowtail butterfly. Found in shady ravines, forest and chaparral. Drought-tolerant; may need occasional water. Does best in part shade.

Leafy Reed Grass
Calamagrostis foliosa

Silvery green bunchgrass that forms beautiful arching clumps. Plume-like, bright yellow-gold flower. The seed-heads attract birds. An uncommon plant in California in the outer North Coast Ranges, North Coast bluffs and cliffs and coastal scrub. Grows in sun or shade; in sun, needs water.

Currant
Ribes sanguineum glutinosum

Shrub growing to 6' by 6'. Pink flowers in late winter, early spring are followed by blue-black berries in fall. The flowers attract hummingbirds. The berries are eaten by small animals and birds. Found along the coast and in North Coast Ranges from central California to British Columbia.

Ithuriel's Spear
Triteleia laxa

Bulb that grows to 12" tall. Large, loose umbels of blue-purple flowers from March to June. Native to northwestern and central western California, Cascade Range, Sierra Nevada, Transverse Ranges and southwestern Oregon in open forest, woodland and grassland in clay soil. Needs sun and summer drought.

CURRANT

LEAFY REED GRASS

MAKING NATURE A PART OF DAILY LIFE

BY ANDY RICE

UST ABOUT EVERYBODY remembers being exhilarated by a vibrant setting in the natural landscape. How many times has the sight of a meadow of wildflowers in every color of the rainbow, or sunlight filtering through conifers into a glade alive with anemones and dogwood made you ask, "Why can't this be an everyday experience?" Well, to a large extent it can. Maybe not on the scale of many wilderness settings. But song sparrows and thrushes, the fragrance of wild mock orange and a rainbow of vine maple in the fall are easily within your grasp.

If provided the right soils and exposure, most Northwest native plants will thrive in garden settings west of the Cascade Mountains. Many of our natives are as spectacular as the best exotic ornamental plants. When combined in ways that approximate natural plant associations in their native habitats, they provide a garden that is attractive throughout the year. Because they're adapted to our climate, they don't require a lot of care; once established, natives are able to cruise through our usually dry summer and fall days without irrigation.

The garden plan on page 98 transforms a typical water-intensive ornamental landscape into a garden that conserves precious water and is both biodiverse and beautiful. Several native plant compositions are represented in the new plan: wetland, Douglas fir woodland, alder wood, oak prairie and Cascade slope. Not all of the plants in each habitat are always found together in the wild; but because they require similar conditions, they can be combined successfully in the garden.

Urbanization and agriculture in the Pacific Northwest have drastically diminished wetland and prairie habitat and their associated vegetation and wildlife. Gardeners can reverse this trend by creating more of this habitat in the built environment.

The range of plants in the plan provide food, shelter and nesting sites for many birds and small creatures. The plants are arranged in ways that attend to human needs, too — by, for example, creating private outdoor living spaces screened from the neighbors and the road. A few brush piles and compost sites, a stump and an old snag or two will provide additional protection for wildlife. Vines like orange honeysuckle and bigroot (*Marah macrocarpus*) will cover the brush piles in summer.

WETLAND

More than half of all plants and animals in the Northwest are found in riparian (streamside) habitats. Consequently, to create the most biodiverse garden it makes sense to enhance or even create conditions favorable for this habitat by

A BIODIVERSE GARDEN FOR THE PACIFIC NORTHWEST

Urbanization and agriculture in the Northwest have drastically diminished wetlands and prairies and their vegetation and wildlife. The plan below reverses this trend by re-creating these habitats. Wetlands are also where more than half the region's plants and animals are found, so they should be a part of any biodiverse garden. Other native plant communities included in the garden design are Douglas fir woodland, alder wood and Cascade slope, an assemblage of species found in foothills and mid-elevation mountain habitats.

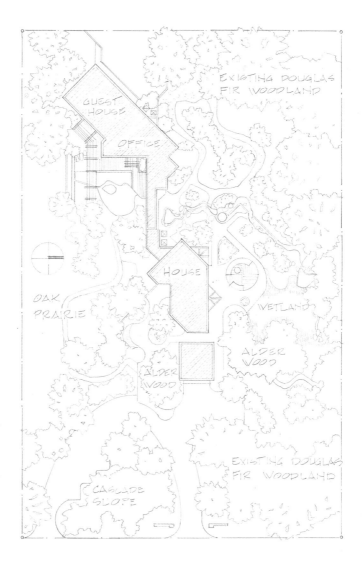

SELECTED NATIVE PLANTS

DOUGLAS FIR WOODLAND:

Vine Maple *Acer circinatum*
Pacific Dogwood *Cornus nuttallii*
Douglas Fir *Pseudotsuga menziesii*
Salal *Gaultheria shallon*
Cascades Oregon Grape *Berberis nervosa*
Red Huckleberry *Vaccinium parvifolium*
Western Sword Fern *Polystichum munitum*
Oregon Wood-sorrel *Oxalis oregana*
Inside-out flower *Vancouveria hexandra*
Bleeding-heart *Dicentra formosa*
Trillium *Trillium ovatum*
Vanilla Leaf *Achlys triphylla*

ALDER GROVE:

Red Alder *Alnus rubra*
Vine Maple *Acer circinatum*
Western Red Cedar *Libocedrus decurrens*
Pacific Yew *Taxus brevifolia*
Pacific Ninebark *Physocarpus capitatus*
Osoberry *Oemleria cerasiformis*
Bush Honeysuckle *Lonicera involucrata*
Goatsbeard *Aruncus dioicus*
Nootka Rose *Rosa nutkana*
Western Sword Fern *Polystichum munitum*
Dewberry *Rubus ursinus*
Coltsfoot *Petasites frigidus*
Douglas Hawthorn *Crataegus douglasii*
Thimbleberry *Rubus parviflorus*
Red-flowering Currant *Ribes sanguineum*
Oval-leaved Viburnum *Viburnum ellipticum*
Red Elderberry *Sambucus racemosa*

OAK PRAIRIE:

Garry Oak *Quercus garryana*
California Black Oak *Q. kelloggii*
Ponderosa Pine *Pinus ponderosa*
Pacific Madrone *Arbutus menziesii*
Oregon Grape *Mahonia aquifolium*
Snowberry *Symphoricarpos albus*
Serviceberry *Amelanchier alnifolia*
Mock Orange *Philadelphus lewisii*
Shrub Tanoak *Lithocarpus densiflorus echinoides*

Ocean-spray *Holodiscus discolor*
Shrubby Cinquefoil *Potentilla fruticosa*

CASCADE SLOPE:

Vine Maple *Acer circinatum*
Douglas Maple *A. glabrum douglasii*
Mountain Hemlock *Tsuga mertensiana*
Lodgepole Pine *Pinus contorta*
Pacific Silver Fir *Abies amabilis*
Salal *Gaultheria shallon*
Sitka Alder *Alnus sinuata*
Subalpine Spirea *Spiraea densiflora*
Bunchberry Dogwood *Cornus canadensis*
Goldthread *Coptis laciniata*
Western Sword Fern *Polystichum munitum*
Baneberry *Actaea rubra*
False Spikenard *Smilacina racemosa*
Snow Queen *Synthyris reniformis*
Western Larch *Larix occidentalis*
Mountain Ash *Sorbus sitchensis*
Oregon Box *Paxistima myrsinites*
Golden Chinquapin *Chrysolepis chrysophylla*
Pacific Rhododendron *Rhododendron macrophyllum*

WETLAND:

Creek Dogwood *Cornus sericea*
Scouler's Willow *Salix scouleri*
Salmonberry *Rubus spectabilis*
Devil's Club *Oplopanax horridus*
Monkey-flower *Mimulus guttatus*
Columbine *Aquilegia formosa*
Camas *Camassia quamash*
Cow Parsnip *Heracleum lanatum*
Umbrella Plant *Peltiphyllum peltatum*
Maidenhair Fern *Adiantum pedatum*
Chain Fern *Woodwardia fimbriata*
Bugbane *Cimicifuga laciniata*
False Lily-of-the-valley *Maianthemum dilatatum*
False Hellebore *Veratrum californicum caudatum*

improving the soil's ability to retain moisture or adding areas of standing and flowing water. In such a setting you're likely to see a ruby-throated humming-bird's dramatic mating dives from the top of a thicket of ninebark, Oregon grape and currant.

In this garden, soil drainage in some locations has been a year-round prob-lem. Instead of regrading, replacing soils or installing subsurface drainage, the new plan embraces this "problem," incorporating natives found naturally in these conditions — sedges and rushes, umbrella plant, lingonberry, wild lily-of-the-valley, lady fern, salmonberry and skunk cabbage, to name a few. We also enhanced an existing water course with a series of pools, adding a boggy area and planting riparian species throughout. Many wildflowers min-gle along the watercourse. Punctuating the planting is the bright yellow com-mon monkey-flower, scattered among dense, dark green blankets of wild lily-of-the-valley.

DOUGLAS FIR WOODLAND

To the north of the wetland area is a mature, second-growth Douglas fir forest. This woodland contains many vine maples, which range widely in search of the filtered sunlight that finds its way through the dense fir canopy high above. The forest floor is a patchwork of early-blooming wood trilliums, followed by vanilla leaf and inside-out flower. Out of this carpet rise sword and wood ferns and red huckleberry, often as solitary specimens. This vegetation has been extended into the new landscape, making the watercourse look all the more natural.

If you want to create a woodland and there are no mature trees on the site, plant fast-growing species like red alder. These will quickly provide shade and nutrients needed by the understory plants such as bleeding-heart, maidenhair fern and salal, a broad-leaved evergreen that will keep the woodland looking lush even under leafless trees on gray winter days.

ALDER WOOD

The light-gray bark and rust-colored catkins of red alder in crystalline winter sunlight are a glorious sight along many western valley byways. While light under the evergreen canopy of Douglas fir woodland is subdued, an alder wood is bright. Even on cloudy summer days with the trees in full foliage, the under-story seems illuminated, with the light-gray trunks often ascending at an angle

The Pacific Northwest includes some of the world's most magnificent forests.

out of light-green drifts of coltsfoot, bleeding-heart and wood sorrel. This natural picture is re-created on a smaller scale in alder groves at the front entry of the house and in areas bordering wetter soils. A few vine maples, western red cedars and yews complement the alders. Evergreen understory plants such as salal, sword fern and evergreen huckleberry, along with creek dogwood with its red stems and red elderberry with its colorful fruits, make this landscape attractive even in the more barren seasons.

OAK PRAIRIE

South of the house are areas where surface slope and soil porosity assure good drainage. Here are the oak prairie and Cascade slope communities, comprising species that thrive in similar conditions on mountain slopes and valley drylands. The oak prairie is planted with native bunchgrasses and wildflowers and bordered by Garry oaks. A walk through such a meadow, with its ever-changing colors and textures, is especially delightful in spring and early summer. Prairie meadow is a magnet for hummingbirds and butterflies, which pollinate and help maintain the wildflower populations.

CASCADE SLOPE

The Cascade Slope comprises plants often found not only in valleys but also foothills and mid-mountain elevations up to 4,500 feet from northern California to southern British Columbia. The garden plan provides a setting for some of the choice conifers, broad-leaved evergreens and perennials found in this plant community. Blue-flowered snow queen peeks through the occasional February or March snow, while smiling sessile trillium and nodding trout lilies appear in April and dainty, yellow-flowered fairy lanterns in May.

Pots and troughs placed in sunny spots around the house provide a home for some of the Northwest's striking but fussy alpines, including saxifrages, lewisias, mountain avens, low mountain lupine and penstemons, where they can be viewed close up. The triangular planting space beside the round wood deck, located near the kitchen, is reserved for culinary herbs.

Devil's club and lupine are a striking combination for a Northwest garden.

AMERICAN BEAUTIES

Mountain Hemlock
Tsuga mertensiana

One of the most elegant native conifers, found above 3,000'. Seldom exceeds 50' tall in cultivation. Grayish to glaucous green needles surround the stems. Well drained soils are essential. For successful transplanting, should be container grown in humus-rich soil and roots should not be disturbed.

Vine Maple
Acer circinatum

A small tree growing to 25'. Found west of the Cascades, usually as a striking, multi-stemmed clump. Younger stems vary from green to reddish, becoming smooth and gray with age. Wine-red flowers in April. Fiery fall leaf color. Rangy in shade, fairly compact in full sun.

Devil's Club
Oplopanax horridus

Occurs mostly at mid-elevations in damp, shaded glades. Spiny stems often to 6' and occasionally 9' topped with leaves up to 12" across. Eye-catching year-round, featuring the stout spiny stems in winter, bold leaves in summer and clusters of red berries in fall. Requires damp humus-rich soil and afternoon shade.

VINE MAPLE

MOUNTAIN HEMLOCK

PACIFIC NINEBARK

Pacific Ninebark
Physocarpus capitatus
A medium-sized shrub of western valleys and coastal areas. Grows to 12' tall. Showy clusters of white flowers in spring. Muted reddish foliage color in autumn. Exfoliating orange-brown and white bark on mature stems is striking in winter. Thrives in moist soils. A preferred nesting site for a variety of birds.

Western Sword Fern
Polystichum munitum
In the deep shaded valley woodlands or sunny cut-over areas, thrives in all but the wettest soils. Splendid cinnamon-colored fiddleheads become dark, leathery, evergreen fronds as much as 5' long. Along with Douglas fir, this is an integral part of the vibrant green characteristic of much of the Pacific Northwest.

Pacific Madrone
Arbutus menziesii
Broad-leaved evergreen tree 20' to 70' tall. Found west of the Cascades. Satiny, orangish to chartreuse bark on young branches, becoming reddish brown and flaky when mature. Clusters of white, urn-shaped flowers in late spring. Red berries beloved by birds. Sun, good drainage and summer dryness are essential.

PACIFIC MADRONE

Pacific Bleeding-heart

Dicentra formosa

When given shade and rich, moist soil, produces little pinkish "dutchman's breeches" blooms from April into late summer. There's also a white-flowering form. Glaucous-green filigreed foliage is attractive until it yellows and withers in the fall. Found west of the Cascades to the coast.

Oregon Iris

Iris tenax

Delightful iris with grass-like foliage, frequently seen on roadside cuts, in pastures and along fence rows. Mid-spring flowers are usually lavender-blue to purple and occasionally white on stems up to 16" tall. A variety, *I. tenax gormanii*, has yellow flowers. Needs a well-drained, sunny site.

Subalpine Spirea

Spiraea densiflora

Although several garden-worthy spireas are native to the Northwest, this one is choice, with its pink- to rose-colored flowers and relatively compact growth habit. A source of food and shelter for birds. Prefers sun and moist soil but tolerates drier conditions.

SUBALPINE SPIREA

OREGON IRIS

CONTRIBUTORS

KAREN BLUMER is a plant ecologist, landscape designer and freelance writer. She is the author of *Long Island Native Plants for Landscaping: A Source Book*, (Growing Wild Publications, Box 275, Brookhaven, NY, $12.95).

C. COLSTON BURRELL is a garden designer, writer, photographer and life-long native plant enthusiast. He is President of Native Landscape Design and Restoration, Ltd. of Minneapolis, Minnesota, a design firm specializing in the creation of environmentally appropriate gardens and ecological restorations.

NEIL DIBOLL is president of Prairie Nursery, provider of native plants and seeds for prairies, meadows, wetlands and woodlands. For a two-year subscription to Prairie Nursery's 48-page color catalog, send $3 to Box 306, Westfield, WI 53964 or call 1-800-GRO-WILD.

RON LUTSKO, JR. is principal of Lutsko Associates, Landscape Architects, a San Francisco design firm specializing in projects that explore the relationship between people and the environment. These projects have been published in a range of books and magazines and have received numerous local and national awards.

JANET MARINELLI is the editor of this handbook and wrote the chapter "What is a Biodiverse Garden?" She is the editor of Brooklyn Botanic Garden's 21st-Century Gardening Series and the author of *The Naturally Elegant Home: Environmental Style* (Little, Brown and Company).

ROBYN S. MENIGOZ is a landscape architect based in Novato, California. She has designed many award-winning gardens in the San Francisco Bay Area, all with a focus on native plants and habitats.

ANDY RICE, a landscape architect for 25 years, hangs his shingle in Lake Oswego, Oregon. His special interests include native and unusual ornamental plants, water gardens and the rural landscape.

JANE SCOTT is the author and illustrator of *Field and Forest: A Guide to Native Plant Communities for the Gardener and Naturalist* (Walker and Company) and several other books on natural history and gardening with native plants for both adults and children.

CAROL SHULER is president of C.F. Shuler, Inc., a landscape architecture firm in Scottsdale, Arizona. Since 1970, she has provided consulting services in Arizona, Nevada and California. She applies the principles of horticulture and ecology in every design.

GEORGIA TASKER is the garden writer for the *Miami Herald*. She is the author of *Enchanted Ground: Gardening with Nature in the Subtropics* (Andrews & McNeel) and *Wild Things: The Return of Native Plants* (Florida Native Plant Society*)*.

SALLY WASOWSKI is a Dallas-based landscape designer and author. Her books include: *Native Texas Plants* (Gulf), *Requiem for a Lawnmower* and *Gardening with Native Plants of the South* (Taylor), and *Native Landscapes: El Paso to L.A.* (Clarkson N. Potter).

GAYLE WEINSTEIN is owner of Eletes Consultants, a Denver firm that specializes in regional, ecological and water-conserving landscape design. She also serves as consulting director of education at Bernheim Arboretum and Research Forest in Kentucky.

ILLUSTRATION CREDITS

Drawings by Jeff Wilkinson. Photos: cover and pages 7a, 43b, 45a, 46, 51a, 51b, 52, 53a, 53b, 54a, 55a, 55b by C. Colston Burrell. Pages 6, 7b, 21, 23a, 24a, 25b, 32, 36, 41, 64b, 70, 80, 83b, 92, 96, 101 by Susan Roth. Page 24b by Stephen Tim. Page 25a by Kerry Barringer. Pages 26, 30 by Georgia Tasker. Pages 33, 34, 35 by Roger Hammer. Pages 43a, 44b, 73a, 75a, 103b by Pamela Harper. Pages 54b, 105a by Jerry Pavia. Pages 56, 60, 61, 62, 63, 64a, 65 by Andy Wasowski. Pages 73b, 74a, 104b by Joanne Pavia. Pages 76, 81, 83a, 84, 85 by Carol Shuler. Page 86 by D. Carrillo. Pages 66, 71, 74b by Gayle Weinstein. Pages 91, 93b, 94a, 95, 104a, 105b by Ted Kipping. Pages 93a, 94b by Ron Lutsko. Pages 102, 103a by Andy Rice. Pages 1, 13, 16, 44a, 63b, 75b by Ken Druse. Pages 23b, 45b by Karen Blumer.

I N D E X

American Cottage Gardening

Annuals: A Gardener's Guide

Bonsai: Special Techniques

Culinary Herbs

The Environmental Gardener

Ferns

Garden Photography

The Gardener's World of Bulbs

Gardening for Fragrance

Gardening in the Shade

Gardening with Wildflowers & Native
   Plants

Greenhouses & Garden Rooms

Herbs & Cooking

Herbs & Their Ornamental Uses

Hollies: A Gardener's Guide

Indoor Bonsai

Japanese Gardens

Natural Insect Control

The Natural Lawn & Alternatives

A New Look at Vegetables

A New Look at Houseplants

Orchids for the Home & Greenhouse

Ornamental Grasses

Perennials: A Gardener's Guide

Pruning Techniques

Roses

Soils

The Town & City Gardener

Trees: A Gardener's Guide

Water Gardening

The Winter Garden

21st-Century Gardening Series

For centuries, gardens have been islands of beauty and tranquility in an often disorderly, unpredictable world. The late-20th-century garden is also a major arena in the struggle to balance human and ecological needs, one of the great tasks of our time. Brooklyn Botanic Garden's 21st-Century Gardening Series explores the frontiers of ecological gardening. Each volume offers practical, step-by-step tips on creating environmentally sensitive and beautiful gardens for the 1990s and the new century.

TO SUBSCRIBE OR ORDER:

21st-Century Gardening Guides are published quarterly — spring, summer, fall and winter. A four-volume subscription is included in BBG subscribing membership dues of $25 a year. Mail your check to Brooklyn Botanic Garden, 1000 Washington Avenue, Brooklyn, NY 11225.

For information on how to order any of the handbooks listed at left, call (718) 622-4433.